Advance Praise for *The Lea...*

"This work is an amazing guide on leadership by one of the most talented, intelligent, and courageous educational leaders I've ever known. Yvonne Caamal Canul's vast experience and student focus shines through in every chapter. Yvonne's reflections are especially powerful. What a wonderful book for both aspiring and practicing educational leaders."
–Mike Flanagan, Michigan's Superintendent of Public Instruction, 2005–2015

"I just want to congratulate my good friend Yvonne. Thank you for making the Lansing School District better. You made sure the kids were getting an excellent education. But, what I really love about you is the fact that you called me up and said, 'Earvin, I need you to be involved in the Lansing Promise and let's send a lot of kids to college.' We have accomplished that and now those kids can get a quality education in college and then go on and have a great career and a great life. That's all because of you. God Bless you."
–Earvin "Magic" Johnson, Graduate Lansing Everett High School, World Famous Athlete, Philanthropist, and Entrepreneur, President and CEO of Magic Johnson Enterprises

"It is easy to forget that public education is just that: a big public business that must find common ground among diverse stakeholders to deliver successfully a public good. Yvonne's 3R's framework will guide leaders — established and emerging — in their efforts to give children and youth (aka our nation's seed corn!) a quality education in a time fraught with issues dividing our states and our communities: an ever-worsening pandemic, a declining economy, changing demographics, and challenges testing our democracy.
–Elizabeth 'Betty' Hale, Former President, Institute for Educational Leadership (IEL), Washington, DC

"It has been said that 'wisdom' is the byproduct of knowledge and experience. Caamal Canul provides early career education leaders with clear-eyed wisdom about meeting the challenges of leading schools in these unprecedented times. Drawn from her 45 years of cross-cultural education leadership, she has designed chapters that contain questions that prompt reflection about the values, beliefs, and practices that influence effective leader behaviors."
–Robert J. Monson, Ph.D., Teachers College, Columbia University

"Yvonne understands the importance of leadership skills in whatever role she takes on. Of the three R's of leadership, she describes in the book, building strong relationships is demonstrated throughout with examples of the importance of collaboration. She describes the leadership skills needed to be able to step outside of your comfort zone that will enable you to begin to change, grow, and transform as a leader."
–Sara Magaña Shubel, Ph.D., East Grand Rapids Public Superintendent 2006-2018, ASCD Past-President 2011-2012

"I have had the good fortune to work with educators across the United States and the world. In my travels, I have not come across a Superintendent as well prepared to guide a school district into the 21st century as Yvonne Caamal Canul. She is a thoughtful, erudite, globalist with decades of educational experience. That breadth of vision informs and inspires her educational philosophy. However, what really makes her stand out, are the three traits she writes about in this book because she actually practiced these leadership essentials and provides the reader with real-life examples of their meaning. I highly recommend this book for educators looking for critical and much needed 21st century leadership traits and skills."
–Joe Carvin, President and CEO, One World

"Over nearly two decades of working with public school superintendents this is the first book I have read that fills a void and serves as a practical guide for anyone aspiring to one of the most difficult roles in America—school administration. But this is also the rare book about servant leadership that could only be written by someone who has practiced it with fidelity for decades, a book I would put on the must-read list of every CEO."
–Suhail Farooqui, Chief Executive Officer, K12 Insight

"Former superintendent of schools, state department of education official and nationally recognized for leadership and innovation, Yvonne Caamal Canul draws on her expertise and rich international and cross-cultural experiences to produce the leadership guide needed by today's educational leaders. Through examples, stories, activities and tools she provides valuable resources to launch and even retool an administrative career. *The Leadership Passcode: Reflection, Relationships, Rituals — Unlock the Heart of School Leadership* is a must-have for both new and veteran leaders. Well done!"
–Rossi Ray-Taylor, PhD, Ray-Taylor and Associates, LLC

"*The Leadership Passcode* is an excellent read. Yvonne Caamal Canul, a veteran education leader, provides visionary thinking, practical strategies, and personal stories about leadership in the most challenging contexts of education."
–Yong Zhao, Ph.D., Foundation Distinguished Professor, School of Education, University of Kansas and Professor in Educational Leadership, Melbourne Graduate School of Education

"What a great way to inspire, encourage and empower excellence! The depth and richness of Dr. Caamal Canul's leadership experiences are expertly displayed on the pages of this book. As a beacon of light they will guide and support the work of innovative administrators across our nation. A must read!!!!!"
–Rosa S. Atkins, Ed. D. , Division Superintendent, Charlottesville City Schools

The Leadership Passcode

MISSION POINT PRESS

Published by Mission Point Press
2554 Chandler Rd.
Traverse City, MI 49696
(231) 421-9513

www.MissionPointPress.com

ISBN: 978-1-950659-99-9
Library of Congress Control Number: 2021901905

Printed in the United States of America

The Leadership Passcode

Unlock the Heart of School Leadership

Yvonne Caamal Canul

Mission Point Press

Dedicated to
Jane (Giovanna Linda DeMaso DeLorenzo) Goudreault.

"You never know where you plant a seed."

Contents

Chapter Three: Rituals

Chapter Three Activities: 1–9

Growth Plans

Appendix: More Thoughts on Leadership

References

Reflection

Relationships

Rituals

Introduction

There are hundreds, no, thousands, of books on leadership dating as far back as the Chinese philosopher Confucius. I suspect even the Neanderthals provided leadership advice in the cave paintings of northern Spain. Amazon alone has over 50,000 books on leadership. Why on earth would we need another one?

I have read many books on leadership during my 45-year career as an educator. Most of them were pretty good, provided unique insights, and gave me food for thought. Unfortunately, few of those books' authors had ever been leaders themselves, fewer of them were women, and even fewer were school leaders. Most were out of the corporate or academic world, from "leaning in" to "standing out" or from "tightening the lug nuts" to "eating last." Many researched leadership, wrote about leadership, interviewed leaders about leadership but weren't actually leaders of public schools or school districts.

When I retired from being a long-serving urban superintendent (defying the odds on shelf life), colleagues and friends encouraged me to write a book. Initially, I thought they wanted me to write about my life, which I thought was a little premature! I was raised in Latin America, came from a family of first-generation American polyglots, married a Mexican Mayan (they did not disappear with the Aztecs, who also did not disappear), and at one point in my life, was the chauffeur for a legal cockfighting enterprise in México. That experience taught me a lot about leadership and how to successfully integrate as the only woman in a completely male-dominated environment. I jokingly said that it prepared me well for the work I had as a superintendent. Instead, my friends and colleagues wanted me to write a book about school leadership, which turns out to be about my life anyway, and what I've experienced and learned about leadership, which, according to my mother, started at the young age of four:

> One day the two little boys who lived next door came to her complaining about me bossing them around. She sat me down and said that I should stop telling them what to do because it wasn't nice. According to her, I replied, "Well, if they had any ideas of their own, I wouldn't have to boss them around!"

While working at Michigan State University on a research collaborative in 2012 with the University of North Carolina at Chapel Hill and funded by the W.K. Kellogg Foundation, a member of the local board of education called and asked me to consider being the superintendent on an interim basis. They just needed me for three months to clean things up. This was in the district where I had spent the first 27 years of my career as a teacher, principal, and Director of Curriculum and Assessment. I had then gone on to work at the Michigan Department of Education (MDE) as the Director of the newly formed Office of School Improvement responsible for implementing all of the conditions set out in the No Child Left Behind Act of 2001 and oversaw about 900 million dollars in flow-through to local school districts and organizations. After retiring from the MDE, I was recruited by an education corporation to "fix" their office in the Chicago area, eventually, moving it to the Atlanta headquarters where I was stationed for nearly three years as one of four senior executives responsible for research and innovation. I had always been tapped to start something new, fix something old, or reassemble broken pieces. In short, put order to chaos.

The university life was a wonderful departure from the vortex of corporate work which is also a bit like working in the Palace of Versailles in the 1700s, and I was very much engaged in the research project, but the opportunity to go back home and take on the challenge of reforming a school district seemed more like a calling and less like the "next job."

What I inherited when I became superintendent was a fractured and dysfunctional school district of 27 schools and five operational facilities. Each of them had raised the drawbridge and hunkered down for the duration.

Decisions were made in isolation, localized, and with "tribal survival" a top priority. A weak central office and top-level leadership that was AWOL created a laissez-faire environment. Staff came to work, students came to school, but there was "no joy in Mudville" as was clear from the escalation of declining enrollment. In addition, the district was in a multimillion-dollar operational deficit. The enterprise was so "loosely coupled," to use Richard Elmore's phrase, that there was no "there" there. How would I bring order and structure not to mention hope and vitality to this chaotic situation?

Where was the leadership book on how to change the district's story? As it turns out the story was inside me already. In reflecting upon all the leadership positions I've had in my career, patterns emerged. And that's how I came to choose the structure for this book. After 45 years of putting order to chaos, I have found that there is a twenty-first century version of the three Rs that must be in a leader's portfolio in order to create a meaningful and transformational educational environment. They are:

- Reflection
- Relationships
- Rituals

Note: At the end of each chapter highlighting an "R," several related activities make applicable the content within.

The popular notion is that it takes approximately eight to ten years to turn a district around; slightly less for a school. There are a number of initial actions that need to be taken when reforming a district, many of which fall within the structure mentioned above. In this book, we'll take a deeper dive into the three Rs, but I think it's important to mention a few of these actions since they are ones I focused on when developing the plan for reform.

- Unpack and uncover the operating culture of the district
- Analyze the relationships between leadership, staff, and community
- Interview key people to find pain and pride points
- Study the symbols and identity images projected by the district
- Analyze the allocation of resources–to whom, for what
- Investigate staffing patterns, attrition, and attendance

- Analyze the technology infrastructure
- Evaluate the facility footprint and usage
- Dig into student performance data
- Codify and analyze instructional practices

It was as if I were an archeologist looking for signs of previous life, going through layers of built-up organizational "silt" until I reached the root causes of the dysfunction.

Archeology aside, an educational leader must first know the craft of the core mission—instruction. There are those who believe you can reform an education organization without having been a teacher or an educator. That may be true in some cases; however, the downside of that notion is that the leader will garner little credibility with those responsible for teaching and learning and those people are essential in carrying forward the leader's plan for reform. The plan must be trusted, feasible, strategic, authentic, and inclusive of stakeholders.

Leading a large school district is a bit like leading a corporation, but the clientele is very different. While a large school district can be likened to a corporation in some ways, our mission in this public education enterprise is based on a completely different premise. We are responsible to and for students, families, the community, and to a great extent the host city's economic prosperity and moral welfare. We are taxpayers' fiscal stewards, a pipeline to careers and college, an assemblage point during celebrations and disasters, and we carry the historical narrative of all who have walked our halls, from pre-kindergarten to graduation. We are the single institution that shoulders the burden of developing a citizenry dedicated to the future well-being of a democratic nation.

And now with my retirement comes treasured time to devote to putting it all down in the form of a book that will hopefully help aspiring and current education leaders to continue developing their craft. Little did I suspect when I began writing that we would be in a world order that was almost entirely virtual. Education was primarily meant to be a face-to-face experience. I know some would disagree, but I doubt many of us chose this profession to sit in front of a computer and work with students in a two-dimensional world. I certainly don't reject the value of technology in education. In fact, I was an early adopter. I bought my first "bundle" in 1985, a Mac SE and dot matrix printer! In the mid-1990s, the College of Education at Michigan State University was looking for innovative ways to teach online and I was fortunate to be invited to co-teach a class on school level leadership with a well-regarded avant-garde professor, Dr. Steve Kaagan, now at Climate Interactive. What we discovered was that the online format was good for content instruction, but in the area of human relations, it was flat. It's hard to decipher the "teachable moment" when looking at a gallery of faces on your screen or to convey the subtle nuances of school leadership. That being said, much of the content in this book can be modified for the current virtual context, if desired. When we return and gather collaboratively and in the presence of each other, I hope the ideas in this book can help restore what might have been lost during the time we were apart.

Acknowledgments

No one develops in isolation. Many people have been instrumental in my journey—some still are, as I continue to grow! By way of this introduction, I'd like to thank a few folks. My first teachers, my parents, Jane (née DeMaso DeLorenzo) and Fernand Goudreault, have passed, but the lessons they taught live on. My gregarious French-speaking father was a risk-taker, my loving Italian-speaking mother was pragmatic. Wherever we called home, visitors knew they would eat well, be appreciated, and be recorded in my mother's address book as lifelong friends. Between them, they raised two kids to be all they could be. I'm so proud of my brother, Paul, an accomplished leader in his own right in the corporate world—calm, introspective, strategic, a great friend, father, and husband. Two maternal aunts, Dora and Delia DeMaso, dedicated teachers in urban schools, influenced the lives of countless disenfranchised children.

Adding to the *smorgasbord of languages* in my life is my husband, Victor. A retired sea captain who, 33 years ago, proved to be right for me because, "if he could handle the sea, he could handle me." He is proud of his Mayan heritage and surname. Years ago, he introduced me to his grandmother who spoke little Spanish but knew enough to say, when she looked at the tall American next to the slightly shorter Mayan, "Victor, Victor, Victor. *Está grande el mueble.*" Translation: "That is one big piece of furniture!" At times, he has lived in my shadow, but he has also created his own path next to mine; always supportive, encouraging, and teaching me to observe more and talk less. My "sister" and best friend, Betty Underwood, is the better half of my conscience, someone with whom I've shared many adventures. She was instrumental in providing encouragement, insight, and ideas for this book. We met as teachers in 1976 at an end-of-school-year event, she in a miniskirt and platform heels, me in bib overalls and sandals. Surprisingly, we decided to go to Mexico together to visit the Mayan ruins. Four decades later, we're still exploring.

Throughout my career, countless people have shaped my sense of self as a professional. Ricardo Briones first hired me; Argelio Pérez and Richard Letts mentored me; Dr. Saturnino Rodríguez provided me with new opportunities to grow; Dr. Richard Halik promoted and guided me; Alda Henderson, Dr. Eva Evans, and Margaret Groves who, without knowing, were role models.

A significant part of a leader's success is the team that joins the journey. I have been blessed with four incredible teams: At the Center for Language, Culture, and Communication Arts—Sharon, Tara, Jan, Sandra, Elda, Nafisa, Shafika, Hanh, Hang, Manivong, James, and Lao; at the Michigan Department of Education—Betty, Joann, Debra, Mark, Mike, Jan, Margaret, and the Lindas; in the Lansing School District—Teresa, Mark, Delsa, Eldon, Bob, Camela, Sam, Jessica, Karlin, Ben, Cordelia; and a dedicated group from the Lansing Board of Education—Peter, Gabrielle, Rachel, Nino, Missy, Bryan, Myra, Nathan, Amy, Guillermo, and Shirley. They all stood with me, taught me much, and will forever be cherished.

I owe much gratitude to colleagues who generously helped me in framing and editing the content presented in this book. My good friend, Sharon Peck, who wrongly (my opinion) decided to move back to Seattle several years ago, is a thoughtful and kind soul (who mourns the death of semicolons) and has been a great counterpart to my sometimes sharp-edged way of viewing the world. We worked together for many years. She knows me well and has gifted me hours of literary support and suggestions, over the phone, even with Franny the cat's frequent interruptions.

Joann Neuroth elevates all thinking by looking at things quietly through squinching laser-like eyes, her Quaker worldview brings balance to my brisk approach to goal achievement. Kate McNenly is an incredibly creative mind who has the uncanny ability to see beyond words by extracting the power of images in creating identity. Dr. Tom Buffett with whom I have lovingly wrangled for many years about the core mission of leadership, provided gravitas to my observations.

In leadership, good friends are hard to find, long-lasting ones, even harder. I am fortunate to count among them those good folks who were kind enough to endorse this book. Key influencers in my life are Jan Urban-Lurain, a great synthesizer and by far the best facilitator I know; Suhail Farooqi, a brilliant conversationalist who ups my game every time we chat; Jerry Swartz and Dr. Malverne Winborne provide an angled view of things few can see; and, Mike Flanagan, a political genius whose leadership as the Superintendent of Public Instruction for Michigan elevated the educational discourse. There aren't enough *thank-yous* for Teresa Szymanski who retired as the city's Chief of Police and joined me in the mission of district reform. I could not have done it without her deep knowledge of the community and "get it done" attitude. Heartfelt appreciation for the friendships of Dr. Sharon Ritchie who gave me a chance to soar again when others might not have; Dr. Michael Rice with whom verbal sparring in any language is cerebral aerobics; Dr. Charles Tucker always stood by me during rough going; Ray Telman for enabling me to expand my leadership reach; and, Bob Kolt made me look better and smarter than I really am. Muchas Gracias to "*mi familia postiza*": Ricardo, Patricia, Reniero, Blanca, Nino, Margarita, and Dave—45 years together and counting!

Who can live without great authors to broaden one's horizons and enjoy a turn of phrase? My favorites are: Isabel Allende, Anchee Min, Arturo Pérez-Reverte, Ken Follett, Ildefonso Falcones, Lisa See, Barbara Kingsolver, Reies López Tijerina, Carlos Castañeda, N. Scott Momaday, Vine DeLoria, Sherman Alexi, J.D. Salinger. To open one's thinking from academic minds: Edgar Schein, Geert Hofstede, Sonia Nieto, Isabel Wilkerson, Cornel West, Rodolfo Acuña, my friend Yong Zhao, and all the references listed throughout the book.

Many thanks to Mission Point Press for agreeing to take on my project and to Doug Weaver, Heather Shaw, Darlene Short, and the MPP staff for their insightful feedback. Their generous and precise focus on finding ways to improve my narrative is greatly appreciated.

My sincerest appreciation goes out to educators around the world who face the daily challenge of creating a caring community in places where communities have imploded, inspiring young minds to be hopeful about their futures when few others are, and for seeing beyond the politics of bureaucracy that tend to make the education enterprise more about accountability and less about the human factor. Leaders who aspire to take on this challenge are unique in our world and should be given a standing ovation.

Reflection

CHAPTER I

Reflection

INTRODUCTION

"We do not learn from experience...we learn from reflecting on experience." John Dewey

We begin this book on leadership with Reflection because everything you do as a leader is either a reflection of who you are and/or a product of your reflection on it. Margaret Wheatley, author of Leadership and the New Science: Discovering Order in a Chaotic World (2006), is one of the world's greatest thinkers on organizational theory and leadership and offers an interesting and helpful perspective on the importance of reflection: "Without reflection, we go blindly on our way, creating more unintended consequences, and failing to achieve anything useful."

We start with four fundamental questions:

- Who am I?
- What's my purpose, my why?
- What happens here?
- What does it mean?

Before any adventure in leadership begins, you need to know who you are as a person and as a leader. Knowing yourself well enables you to find threads of commonality with others and therefore build the trust needed to bring your vision forward. It's not easy for people to follow a leader that they don't know or trust. Therefore, an essential strategy for gaining that trust is to share with them who you are. Of course, in order to do that, you must first be clear about your own strengths and challenges. In the process of self-discovery, you may find that the mantle of leadership is not compatible with your personal strengths or challenges. Alternatively, you may realize that your strengths closely match those that are likely to translate into a rewarding career in school leadership. We will spend a good amount of time in this chapter exploring Who Am I? Knowing and understanding who you are is foundational for all leadership behavior.

Knowing why you've chosen this path of leadership is essential. Being a leader is hard and lonely work. If you're not clear about why you're doing this, you will easily fall into the rut of "sticking it out" until retirement. If others perceive you as that kind of leader, it will be difficult to engage and move your community forward. They may think that your vision is about self-preservation and not about the good of the community. Is your purpose about building a nest egg or about impacting change? Have you decided to take the leadership path because someone told you to? Is the title important? Are you looking for a new challenge? Do you see it as a calling? You should be clear about the reason why you have decided to go down this road because there will be times when it's bumpy and you will need to have your purpose well rooted in order to get through the rough stretches.

In this chapter, we will also explore the importance of analyzing and reflecting upon the organization's context and the data that illustrates that context.

The great Brazilian philosopher, Paulo Freire, often used the word "praxis" to define a quality of leadership—Action, Reflection, Action (1970). The cycle of decision-making involves deep reflection upon an action and then acting upon that reflection. If you can't ask good questions about the current context or the data it represents, you will miss the opportunity to make better decisions. Why are we doing this? Is it because we've always done it this way? Are there data to support this decision? Is there another way to approach this problem? What do stakeholders think? What does it mean to the community if we decide to do it in this way? Who are they and how are they affected? These questions are important for thoughtful reflection and can serve as a foundational element of your leadership, especially as you lead and mentor your team.

As you move through the content and activities in this book, spend some time reflecting upon the examples that resonate with your own experience and context. Each leader lives in a unique space and time along a continuum of personal and professional development that builds on every learning experience. If we don't take the time to reflect on those learning moments, we are just going through the motions without purpose, without passion, and without a vision for a desired future.

Who Am I?

If you do not know yourself as a leader, no one else will either—or, worse, others will invent a persona that is not who you are. Knowing your leadership style is fundamental to your work. Many good leadership typology inventories can help you explore your personal style. Each one has a unique way of interpreting your style (and your staff's) and can help you better understand who you are, what challenges you might face in developing your leadership vision or in addressing issues with your staff. Don't be afraid to explore all of them. (A list of inventories can be found in the Activity Section at the end of this chapter.) Discovering your typology can help answer many questions about why and how you approach life. Unpacking my typology through the Myers-Briggs Type Indicator (MBTI) answered so many questions like why I was more interested in big ideas than rules. Or, why I preferred to chat with a few people, instead of mingling with many at parties. Or, even why I am comfortable with change when others are not. The results can be illuminating and extremely important as you reflect upon the ways in which you approach your plan of action in implementing your leadership vision.

When I stepped in as the superintendent of a district in chaos, the need for reform was clear. However, reform requires "change" and change is hard for many. In order to bring the administrators on board with the reform efforts, first we needed to analyze who we were and how that would affect our ability to effectively change. As an activity, I administered the Keirsey Temperment Sorter (similar to MBTI) to the entire administrative staff. What we discovered was that 78 percent of them were Guardians! This is not uncommon for folks in the education profession. Change was going to be hard for them. The information gathered provided a great opportunity for us to explore ways in which we could launch our reform strategies by acknowledging the kinds of challenges we would face together along the way.

As a woman leader, knowing your typology is instrumental in helping negotiate the sometimes-difficult waters in a traditionally male-dominated leadership environment. Based on the MBTI, I am an INTP (Introverted, Intuitive, Thinking, Perceiver). Less than 2 percent of women are INTPs. Women have been traditionally socialized toward "feeling" instead of "thinking." A "thinking" woman is often considered too strident.

Reaching adulthood in the middle of the Equal Rights Amendment (ERA) polemic of the sixties and seventies, it was helpful for me to discover my strengths and challenges as I developed professionally in the institutionally conventional environment of education. Often, I was the only woman on the administrative team. And yet, 40 years later, I was among a handful of female superintendents in the nation and when I was chosen as Superintendent of the Year for Michigan, I was one of only seven other women selected in the nation from their states. I've endured sexist language and behavior and emerged without drowning in self-pity, anger, or revenge. There were times when I had to bite my tongue; other times when I did not. Pick your battles.

One of the hallmarks of leadership is to be able to adapt to the environment without sacrificing your values or creating enmity. Know when to hold them, fold them, and even walk away (thank you Kenny Rogers). The best way to rise above the fray is to know who you are as a leader, stay true to yourself, have a successful career, and leave a positive legacy.

A closing thought about knowing yourself as a leader is to know and understand where you are in terms of the evolution of your leadership growth and where the organization is in its evolutionary cycle. Every leader goes through her/his evolution of development from Emerging to Sundown. Likewise, every organization goes through an evolutionary cycle from Forming to Resigned. Your success as a leader often depends on the right "fit." You hear about fit between a leader and the organization frequently

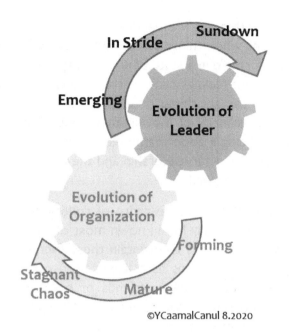

In Stride Sundown

Emerging

Evolution of Leader

Evolution of Organization

Forming

Stagnant Chaos Mature

©YCaamalCanul 8.2020

but it's hard to decipher what exactly "fit" means.

Perhaps the diagram can help you visualize the concept. Would you place an Emerging leader in an organization that is Resigned and in Chaos? Would a Sundown leader want to lead an organization that is just Forming? Take a step back and analyze the organization's (school, district) point on the continuum of its evolution and ask yourself, "Am I at the right stage in my own evolution as a leader to lead this organization?" Even more importantly, is it time for me to move on? At the end of Chapters One and Two there are two activities related to this notion: Evolution of the Leader in Chapter One and Evolution of the Organization in Chapter Two.

Be With and Learn From Others Unlike You

Some leaders have a tendency to surround themselves with like-minded people and enjoy a certain level of comfort by working with people who share their perspective. Who can blame them? There are enough challenges in leadership to deal with and having people on your team who are more like you is one less problem. However, a good leader needs to have a team that will see things from different angles. For example, you might be the kind of leader who is matter-of-fact, anxious to get things done, is practical, and action-oriented. If everyone around you is the same way, you might forget the importance of sending a thank-you or birthday card, providing words of sympathy for a loss, or even publicly sharing a "good job" to someone who's feeling a little disengaged. If you are not that kind of "feeling" leader, you need to have someone close to you or on your team who is.

You might be a person who leads "with a gut feeling." While intuition is sometimes helpful in making decisions when things exist in an ambiguous space, people generally are not comfortable in a state of uncertainty. Intuition rarely comes with solid data so gut feelings can't be the only way to arrive at a decision. Having staff who can get things done in a sequential, timely, and coherent manner is the hallmark of moving an organization forward. Be aware, however, that building a good team takes time and is dependent upon the evolution of not only your leadership and the organization's, but that of your team members as well.

Throughout your career, you will develop a unique cadre of colleagues, acquaintances, and even friends. Many you may have known most of your life. One of the difficult aspects of leadership is to maintain these friendships without them interfering in your decisions as a leader. You can't promote an employee just because you are lifelong friends or because you went to high school with her/his parents. Promotions must be made on merit, not friendship. If you only promote people you like, others will believe they have limited chances of moving up in the organization if they think friendship is the sole criteria. Decisions you make as a leader must be based on evidence of competence.

As a new superintendent in a dysfunctional organizational environment, I needed to assemble a team of people who were well-known and trusted by employees. That meant dipping deeply into the organization and selecting individuals who had been there for many years and who were appreciated for their leadership on a smaller scale. A couple had been my adversaries in another time but I knew them and respected their ability to get things done. Reflecting upon *Team of Rivals: The Political Genius of Abraham Lincoln (2006)* by Doris Kearns Goodwin, the selection wasn't based on friendship. It was far better to have them inside the tent with me. By carefully choosing people who represented various levels of leadership within the district and who had divergent points of view from mine, we could move the district forward with the support of employees and I would gain insight that I might not otherwise have.

Be very analytical about selecting team members closest to you. Think deeply about who they are, what they bring, and what their narrative might be in the organization. You need to trust them. You need to know they won't leave a meeting and subvert decisions made, or do an end run, subverting your leadership. Many times, these appointments have political undertones and you must be very careful about who you select/promote by making sure to use criteria based on the culture of the organization and that of the community.

It's always nice to have everyone agree with you, but it doesn't help much in your quest to be reflective. A team that can politely disagree with you, even if you're the boss, is essential in making sure the decisions you make are faithful to and representative of the well-being of the community you serve and lead. Surrounding yourself with "yes" staff is a sure way to lose the trust and support of your organization's employees, and your image as a leader will be less than desired.

Recently, Michael Kruse wrote an article in Politico (2020) outlining potential downfalls for leaders. This particular quote is very telling when thinking about having some team members unlike oneself:

> "Ted Kennedy once told me a story that I think applies," said longtime Democratic strategist Shrum. "It was the summer of '63, and he was sitting with his brother on the Truman balcony at the White House, and JFK remarked, 'If you ever get to be president, you always have to have two or three or four people around who are allowed to tell you when you're being a dumb SOB–and you have to reward them, not punish them.' Because you will make terrible decisions if you think you are the only one who's right all the time."

Have Friends Who Speak Truth to Power

While it's important to have team members that may not always agree with you, it's also important to have good friends who will speak honestly and candidly. By this time in your career and life, you have likely accumulated a group of friends who have been with you from childhood, school days, college life, social affiliations, and from your profession. Having friends is an important part of enriching one's life. Research indicates that positive relationships actually extend one's life span! Of course, a dog will always listen (cats only when they feel like it!) to your recounting of the day's events, but there's nothing like having a real-life person with whom to dialogue. Malcolm Knowles, world-renowned expert in the field of andragogy (the study of adult learning), said that as we get older, there's a "fanning out" of friendships. Meaning that friends we might have had at one point in our personal and professional development, may not be the same friends we have as we get older or move into subsequent phases of our career and life path. They could still be friends, but the commonality we once had, has "fanned out" to a point where we may not have much in common anymore. That's why it's important to maintain or search for relationships with those with whom you can grow as you continue on your leadership journey.

As a leader, there is no question that you need friends who can make you think, who can converse on a variety of topics, who can enhance your search for deeper knowledge. However, more importantly, do you have friends who will sit you down and tell truths about you that are hard to hear? Friends who speak truth to power? Of course, "power" is a relative term and in this example, it's not about positional power, it's more about one's personal willingness (power) to accept a friend's advice, or not, knowing there is a possibility of sacrificing that friendship.

One day, my best friend invited me to lunch. We sat at a high top table at the Cheesecake Factory and ordered a glass of wine. I could tell there was something on her mind, but at the time, could not have imagined the conversation topic. She very carefully told me that I was not behaving like myself. She warned me that I was making decisions that were not in accordance with my espoused values. She nicely, but very firmly, told me that I needed to dial back my intensity, my arrogance, my impatience. I had a hard time swallowing this at the time but, given the fact that she was speaking her truth and that she was my best friend, I listened and integrated. It was very good advice because she was right.

Every leader needs to have a friend or two who will speak a truth that might not feel good to hear. Your advice to yourself can't be the only advice you hear.

Expand Your Perspective

One of the hallmarks of a great leader is someone who knows her/his craft. Deep knowledge is critical in building the trust you will need to create followers. It's hard to get people to see your vision if you don't know what you're talking about! This does not mean you have to be a renowned researcher or academic from a top-tier university. It does mean that you need to study your profession and reflect upon your decisions as they relate to good practice and explain the rationale behind your decisions to stakeholders. (See Activity Section at the end of this Chapter on Instructional Strategies.)

Many aspiring leaders will exclusively read professional material to improve their understanding of their craft. Reading both nonfiction (professional reading from others' perspectives) and fiction (where characters make choices and live with consequences) is essential for developing yourself as a leader with deep knowledge. To be sure, it is fundamental to stay abreast of new research, emerging policies, and promising practices that are crucial to every aspiring leader. However, much can be learned from a view of the world through the eyes of a different character. Add a bit of fictional reading to your bedside table! Fictional authors provide the reader with a narrative or the turn of phrase that can steadily improve one's vocabulary and ability to communicate with precision and authenticity. Perhaps fiction doesn't explain leadership choices; it lets you live inside the head of a leader, observing how they live their values and agreeing or disagreeing with how they do it.

You may want to step into reading different genres—both in fiction and nonfiction. Some of the best professional books and articles on leadership come from the world of business; other illuminating fictional works on leadership come from unexpected sources. Movies also offer unique insights into leadership behavior. I'm going a bit off the path with this suggestion, but I think Babe is a great leadership movie. Yes, the one about the pig on Mr. Hogget's farm that thinks it's a sheepherding dog.

The dogs on the farm counsel Babe that sheep are stupid and that he needs to dominate them, bend them to his will, accept what he is and be thankful for it. But, Babe is kind to the sheep, asks for their permission to herd them, and thanks them. The sheep love Babe. Babe's owner, Mr. Hogget, notices that Babe has an uncanny ability to get the sheep to do what he asks and decides to sign him up in the big sheepherding competition, exclusively for dogs. However, Babe realizes that the competition sheep are not the same as his friends on the farm and they don't follow his commands. Hogget's alpha male dog, Fly, pleads with the sheep on the farm and is finally given the secret "universal sheep password" which he "barks" to Babe. Success!

The reason why I think this is such a great leadership movie is because Babe doesn't accept what he is, but who he is; he develops relationships with those unlike himself through kindness and curiosity; and, he uses his relationships for a better purpose.

The Importance of Understanding Culture

In order to expand your personal perspective, you will need to expand your worldview. Undoubtedly, one of the most important qualities for a leader is to be culturally competent. We are living in a very "flat" world, right next to people unlike ourselves. Globalization has leveled the playing field (thus making it "flatter") and just because you currently live in a homogeneous environment doesn't mean you'll always be there or that it will eternally remain as such. How would you rate yourself in terms of your cultural intelligence? By getting to know the cultural norms and values of people unlike yourself, you greatly enhance your ability to engage effectively with community constituencies that may not live in an environment quite like yours. If you want to be an effective leader, you can't only have followers who are just like you!

There are many books you can read on cultural competencies and proficiencies; however, one of the best ways to expand your understanding of others is to BE with others. You can also expand your perspective through travel and/or by having a social network of friends and colleagues who are different culturally, linguistically, and racially from you. Remember, EVERYONE has culture. It is not something that only belongs to people in other countries, to those who are from other countries, to a race, or to an ethnicity. We all have cultural "norms, values, standards of behavior that make the actions of the individual intelligible to the group" (Hall 1959). Furthermore, it is essential to understand that nondominant races and cultures must operate within a society where the dominant race has established the acceptable norms and values. Therefore, nondominant races and cultures must adapt in order to survive and function. However, members of the dominant culture and race have the option (and privileged position) of choosing to engage with nondominant communities. Understanding this perspective is crucial for a leader to be able to work with communities unlike their own.

In *Cultural Intelligence* by David Thomas and Kerr Inkson (2017), they propose that in order to have cultural intelligence, you need three competencies: knowledge, mindfulness, and adaptive skills.

- First, the culturally intelligent person requires knowledge of what culture is, how cultures vary, and how culture affects behavior.

- Second, the culturally intelligent person needs to practice mindfulness, the ability to pay attention reflectively and creatively to cues in the situations encountered and to one's own knowledge and feelings.

- Third, based on knowledge and mindfulness, the culturally intelligent person develops cross-cultural skills and becomes competent across a range of situations, choosing the appropriate behavior from a repertoire of behaviors that are correct for a range of intercultural situations. (p. 14)

You can think of personal examples of how these three factors have contributed to your own cross-cultural interactions.

Transmission of Cultural Values

We know from research that cultural and racial perspectives are embedded at a very early age. In the late 1930s, groundbreaking research was done by the team of Drs. Kenneth and Mamie Clark, the results of which were used as evidence in the landmark case before the Supreme Court of Brown v. Board of Education (1954) that "separate but equal" was not only not equal, it was an injustice. Called the "doll test," the research demonstrated the detrimental effects of institutional racism on black children. Other work done by Louise Derman-Sparks, Carol Tanaka Higa, and Bill Sparks in the late seventies, further illustrated this disparity between being a dominant race and not seeing yourself as "racial" in comparison with nondominant races that perpetually see themselves as "racial." (You can find a summary of their research at: www.teachingforchange.org in an article entitled "Children, Race and Racism: How Race Awareness Develops.")

Enculturation of prejudice is generational and passed on to children both implicitly and explicitly. As illustration, observe the lyrics written by Richard Rodgers in 1949 for the very successful Broadway musical, South Pacific. Loosely based on James Michener's novel, *Tales of the South Pacific*, Rodgers and Hammerstein wanted to send a clear, candid, and progressive message on racism.

You've Got to Be Carefully Taught – Richard Rodgers
You've got to be taught
To hate and fear,
You've got to be taught
From year to year,
It's got to be drummed
In your dear little ear
You've got to be carefully taught.
You've got to be taught to be afraid
Of people whose eyes are oddly made,
And people whose skin is a different shade,
You've got to be carefully taught.
You've got to be taught before it's too late,
Before you are six or seven or eight,
To hate all the people your relatives hate,
You've got to be carefully taught!

Analyzing your own cultural biases as a leader is essential in a diverse society. As an educational leader, you are uniquely responsible for ending the cycle of bias transmission in our children.

I spent the better part of my childhood in Latin America (Brazil, México, and Chile) and learned at a very early age to be culturally adaptive.

I am a TCK—Third Culture Kid. TCKs move between cultures before they have had the opportunity to fully develop their personal and cultural identity. Ruth and John Useem studied the effects of the life of a "global nomad" in the 1950s and found that TCKs have "distinct standards of interpersonal behavior, work-related norms, codes of lifestyle and perspectives, and communication creating a new cultural group that does not fall into their home or host culture." When I returned to the US from Chile at the age of 15, the transition to my "home culture" was extremely difficult. The Useems, then at Michigan State University, spent many hours with me asking questions about my life experiences which proved to be extremely helpful in my being able to be comfortable with my own unique identity—quite different from everyone else's who looked like me. I would frequently state that, "Soy güera por fuera." Translation: "I'm white on the outside." In fact, throughout my career, I have found that being a cultural chameleon has had many distinct advantages:

- Expanded worldview knowing that there is more than one way to look at situations.

- Interpersonal sensitivity to a variety of perceptions and lifestyles allowing me to monitor and register societal norms and cues more adeptly.

- Cross-cultural competence or cultural intelligence to function effectively across national, ethnic, and organizational cultures.

However, the TCK phenomena isn't only something that happens when one travels between countries. Many people in our own country live between two worlds. Every day, they step outside their house (one world) and into another. There are many challenges in living between two worlds, and a great leader must not only acknowledge those challenges but also deeply understand them in order to bring a diverse community together for the benefit of all. The advantage of having cultural intelligence in a global society is invaluable. It is important to know how to observe and reflect upon your cultural environment, to understand the cultural cues that are circling about you, and to be able to adapt your own behavior in ways that make your "actions intelligible to the group."

You might think that cultural competency is academic, but there are multiple examples of how people's actions are not intelligible to the group and therefore enable a marginality that delays full participation in a society. A very simple example of this notion appeared on a TV show I like:

The other night I was watching Guy's Grocery Games. Guy Fieri invites four chefs to his "supermarket" to cook in a time-crunching competition. Three culinary judges make the final decision on which chef moves on to the final competition and a monetary award. The other night a new judge was invited. A very young woman who has some notoriety after winning a recent cooking competition joined the veteran judges on the dais. As they tested the dishes before them, she started cutting the long pasta noodles. A shocked Guy Fieri asked her, "Are you cutting the pasta?!" She replied by saying that she didn't want sauce to fly all over herself in front of the TV audience. Guy actually FaceTimed another regular judge, Antonia Lofaso, and shared the news that the new judge was cutting her pasta. Antonia replied, "She's not Italian."

Not paying attention to your cultural environment and not looking for or paying attention to norming cues can lead to an embarrassing situation. The other judges ate the pasta as it was presented (pay attention to the cues around you), most everyone knows that you don't cut your pasta to make it easier to eat—especially on national television (expand your knowledge about cultural norms), and her individual actions were not "intelligible to the group" (adaptive skills). For one small moment, the young pasta-fearing judge could have acted with cross-cultural authenticity by eating the pasta as it was served even at the risk of a splatter, used a napkin, or by being extra careful.

Being culturally adaptive can have a positive impact on your working relationships and success as a leader:

Several years ago, I was working in China. My mission was to secure a memorandum of understanding (MOU) between the corporation for which I worked and a private school company. The owner of the Chinese company and his wife were very hospitable and frequently invited me to dine with them. On one particular evening, the time was set aside for the signing of the agreement with the owner and his entourage. We went to dinner at a very nice restaurant, sat in a private dining room, chatted, and waded through the numerous courses of fantastic dishes selected by the host. The main course was wheeled in with a large covered platter and placed in the center of the round table. The owner lifted the lid and there lay a giant cooked snake, glimmering diamond-patterned skin and all! A delicacy to be sure, but not something I had ever eaten. However, a mission is a mission, and when he served me a big chunk, I ate it smiling. To this day, I don't know if the snake was a special delicacy ordered for the event or a challenge to my sincerity of purpose! The MOU was signed.

A friend asked me if I would have eaten the snake had the stakes not been so high. I replied that when you're in a leadership position, just about everything is "high stakes." That's why leaders need to have a very clear notion of who they are, what they value, with whom they associate or partner, and what they're willing to compromise to accomplish a goal. Making your actions "intelligible to the group" very much depends on who the group is and the purpose of your actions. In the case above, I calculated the risk in not eating the snake and decided that I could still look at myself in the mirror if I indulged. The stakes were high enough and the compromise was small enough that I decided to enter into this cross-cultural space. Actually, the snake wasn't that bad and I was pleased that I could get beyond my own biases to experiment with something unknown to me before.

A great leader is someone who can easily and comfortably move between racial, ethnic, socio-economic, and gender orientation cohorts with authenticity. You can make it clear to everyone where you stand on cultural and racial acceptance through your behavior and actions. There's no place for intolerance, bigotry, or racism in a society comprised of the distinctive richness of humanity.

By exploring, reflecting upon, and understanding your racial, ethnic, or socio-economic biases, you can develop a leadership style for the ages. If you learn (or already know) a different language, you exponentially expand your horizons and understanding of others.

Have a Plan for Atonement

At the end of each day, you should spend a few minutes quietly reflecting upon the day's events, your part in those events, and ways in which you could do better. It's a mental "video-replay" of the day and it's an important routine for every leader who seeks to be reflective. In the hurried chaos of a leader's day, something might have been said that hurt another, done without thinking it through, or completely forgotten. This video-replay provides the leader an opportunity to develop a plan for atonement—to return tomorrow and make things better, to repair a hurt feeling, redo that which had been done poorly, or remember that which had been forgotten.

By reflecting upon your actions at the end of the day, you develop a sense of understanding yourself better. You are reflecting upon your words and actions. You are thinking about them in relationship to the people you are leading, or with those who are leading you. Keep these questions in mind as you video-replay the day:

- What was the first thing I did in the morning?
- With whom did I interact and how did that go?
- Was there someone I should have touched base with that I didn't?
- Did I say something I shouldn't have? Or should have?
- Was I true to my stated values?
- Did I speak the truth?
- Do I feel good about the day I had?
- Is there anything I need to do differently?
- What plan do I have for atonement?

What's My Purpose, My Why?

Simon Sinek (author and motivational speaker) says we should always start with asking "why?" (2011). True enough. However, if you don't know who you are as a leader, your "why" might not come across as authentic! Think about leaders who espouse certain values but don't lead with those values.

Have you ever heard people say, when asked why they chose their profession, "I didn't know what else to do?" Or, "I didn't want to move." Or, "The salary was good." These might be acceptable answers for someone who does not aspire to leadership, but for anyone deciding to move into the very challenging world of leading others, they are not. A leader must know and be clear about why she/he is doing this work. It's more of a calling and less of a job. Dr. Amy Wrzesniewski, professor of Organizational Behavior at Yale University, has researched the world of "job crafting" (2013) and has found that those who find their work meaningful and with purpose are the happiest in life.

You may be tempted to take a job that has all the accessories you want—salary and benefits, close to your home, a worthy title. Resist the temptation to accept if you are not called to the possibilities the job can offer you in making a difference and in advancing your vision for the future of that community. Make sure the people with whom you will work also share your leadership values and are similarly called to their mission.

Several years ago, I was recruited to work in a corporate position that had great salary and benefits, travel to exciting places, a mission of research and innovation in education, and a talented staff. After being there for a while, I began to notice that the leadership style of the person to whom I reported (the CEO) was incongruent with my values of leadership. I found it hard to respect and follow the leader's decision-making approach, treatment of staff with favoritism, and mercurial personality. Being a veteran educator myself, I chose my own direction at times. In retrospect, I took the job because it was a new adventure with great "accessories" but the work environment was difficult and, aside from the accessories, I had little interest in the core mission. For months, I agonized over this situation, even unintentionally sabotaging my own position within the corporation. In the end, my boss and I decided it was a bad match and we amicably parted ways. Even for an experienced professional, it was a tough lesson to learn, but a good lesson.

As Don Juan the Yaqui, from Carlos Castaneda's masterpiece (1968), says, "Follow the path with heart."

Sinek also says that, "People don't follow you because of what you do, they follow you because of why you do it." A leader needs to inspire followers and if you don't know why you are doing what you are doing, then why would anyone WANT to follow you? It's just that simple. The reason why you have chosen to lead is one of the most essential questions you will ask yourself. Being authentic and consistent about this choice is crucial in order to develop your leadership style and vision. The people you are leading are depending on your compass pointing due north, coherent with your "why"; which is also their "why."

As the principal of a wonderful school, I knew my "why." Schooling is a life-altering experience for every child. It can be either positive or negative; students will always remember how they were treated. I believe that school is a place where children can explore their dreams and I would always say to the staff, "We are here for and because of the kids, no matter how they come to us."

There was one teacher who was woefully disorganized and whose classroom was stacked with papers in corners, desks askew, little student work, and no space for kids to "get away." I asked her one day if she could please clean things up and make the room a pleasant environment for the students. She questioned why she should since the kids came from places much worse than her classroom. This is when I almost took off my earrings (urban euphemism for ready for a fight)! I told her that when our babies woke up in the morning, maybe alone or in a bed that was not theirs, they were going to make an important decision every day—do I go to school or stay home and watch TV? And, if what they were coming to wasn't a lot better than what they were leaving, why would they choose to come? Her job was to give those babies the best six-and-a-half hours of the day, every day, so that when they woke up in the morning they couldn't wait to see her.

Your "why" is the reason people will trust you, follow you, and support your leadership vision.

What Happens Here?

As a leader, it is imperative that you find out and ask what is happening here. Many times people just go about their daily routine without stopping to think about what influence their actions might have. That is why it's important to step back with a critical eye and ask yourself and others for a reality check. One of my favorite professors at Michigan State University was Dr. Phil Cusick, now Professor Emeritus, and the author of numerous books on the American high school, used to say that a good leader's mind is like the inside of a flight control tower. All the planes are coming in for a landing or taking off. You have to know where all the planes are and make sure they accomplish their actions successfully. I used to say to teachers that their minds should be like radar, beeping to let them know where all their students are at all times. If you only live within yourself, never ask questions, and have a radar that barely extends six inches from your face, you will not know what's happening here or anywhere else for that matter. We'll spend a good amount of time unpacking this notion in Chapter Three on Rituals.

Several years ago, a select group of veteran educators was hired to work in schools that had been identified as underperforming. They were to spend an entire year in a school, identify the problem areas and reasons for their poor performance on state exams, and co-develop solutions with the school's leadership and staff. The initiative, launched by the Michigan Department of Education, was called Partnership for Success.

One of the first activities in which they were engaged was to ask, "What's Happening Here?" This snapshot of the school environment and symbolic representation of its culture would provide key data on the reasons why the school was underperforming. While effective classroom instruction is key to academic success for students, the environment in which this happens also needs to be a healthy culture. The veteran educators were to analyze not only the physical environment and use of space but to also observe and think about the iconography of the school—display of student work, images of school identity, equitable depiction of cultural diversity. They were to examine classroom instruction and the manner in which students were learning, as well as observe adult interaction, map out classroom and staff meeting locations and spaces for parent engagement, and evaluate the location of the main office. These are all factors a leader must think about and analyze when developing her/his plan of action or reform.

 In one of the schools we worked, staff meetings were held in the first-grade classroom located across the hall from the Principal's office. Teachers had to sit in first-grade chairs at first-grade tables during the meeting. The teacher of that classroom sat at her desk several feet away from the congregated area. The principal conducted the meeting from a first-grade chair. This classroom was also the main storage area for the school's construction paper and Kleenex.

Believe it or not, there are politics involved in these decisions! Every time you ask, "Why are we doing this?", you may ruffle a few feathers. Many stories can be told about WHY "what happens here" gets structured this way. Noting and observing "what is happening here" is thus the deep foundation for the reflection that follows. Here, for instance, are some questions that could grow from that observation:

- Why are staff meetings held in this classroom and not the library down the hall?
  - Think about where you will hold your staff meetings. Neutral areas are best because they do not give the impression that any single staff member is more important than others are.

- Why is the construction paper in that classroom and not in some neutral area in the school in order to access it without disrupting instruction?
  - Staff should not have to interrupt others' instruction (or get permission) to access essential supplies.

- Who is the leader of this school?
  - Everyone is depending on the principal to be the leader. Staff have enough to do with nurturing and teaching students and no single staff

member has the authority to make decisions, other than the principal. Collaboration is key to moving a community forward, but at the end of the day, the principal is the person people look to for the final say.

The question, "What's going on here?" is critical if a leader has a vision for making changes. Never walk in and change things without first analyzing the current cultural context. There are leaders who walk into an organization and immediately make structural, staffing, or cultural changes without first understanding why, who, or what. Use an "environmental scan" *(Activity Section in Chapter Three)* when you arrive, or better yet, before you arrive in your new position (which I did before taking on district reform). Look at the data, demographics, strategic/improvement plan, budget, achievement status, facility footprint, staffing assignments, organizational chart, partnerships with community or business groups, and the overall cultural and political landscape of the environment.

It is hard work, to be sure, but keeping your mission clear and constant by creating an environment of collaborative inquiry and shared decision-making will, over time, embed and sustain your leadership vision. Open discussions that involve some kind of metacognition (thinking aloud) are helpful in garnering trust, engagement, and participation. Find ways to use staff meetings for deep inquiry and analysis instead of checking off the more menial tasks. Remember that getting through an agenda does not imply efficacy.

I remember going to staff meetings as a teacher where the principal would read the rules in the handbook for federal compliance as our meeting content. I thought it was a waste of my time since I could easily read the rules myself. Clearly, this leader did not have a meaningful meeting agenda in mind. When I became a school principal, I fell into the same trap of a meeting "to do" list: distribution of Kleenex, pencils, copy paper; rules for the lounge refrigerator; parking spot assignments, etc. Awful. I knew I had 11 hours of contractual time to use for staff meetings; it was my decision about how to use them. We, the staff and I, decided to use those hours for obligatory professional learning—they chose the learning they wanted or thought they needed. In lieu of the traditional "staff meeting," we convened voluntary school improvement meetings to discuss and decide on the day-to-day issues as they related to the school's operations and strategic plan.

This change created a different narrative for the staff, one of continuous learning where they had input on what they wanted to learn. If they wanted to be involved in the decisions on distribution of Kleenex, they had to attend the voluntary meeting; if not, they had to live with the decisions made there. Continuous learning isn't just for students.

It is impossible to determine what is happening in a school or district without focusing on instruction. That is, after all, the core mission of the enterprise. Unfortunately, historically we have spent too much time analyzing outcome data on high stakes student achievement tests. Generally, the data are a year old, not aligned to instruction, and loosely reflect the performance of students who have moved on to another grade/teacher/city. We can't change the outcomes without changing the process. I had become quite disenchanted with years of analyzing student test data that didn't tell teachers much about how to change their instructional techniques. Before becoming a superintendent, I was fortunate to be a part of a research project led by Dr. Sharon Ritchie at the University of North Carolina at Chapel Hill in partnership with Michigan State University. She had designed a truly groundbreaking classroom observation instrument (EduSnap) that provided both qualitative and quantitative data to help teachers better understand the classroom environment and learning experience for students. The project, First School, funded by the W.K. Kellogg Foundation, had the promise of changing the conversation about process. It was such an innovative way for teachers to dialogue about instruction that when I became superintendent, we implemented the observation protocol in all classrooms throughout the district.

In the fall of 2012, I met with the entire district teaching staff in a bowling alley banquet hall at the beginning of the school year and told them that we were not going to analyze statewide achievement tests anymore. We were going to spend our time looking at instructional processes. While there was a bit of trepidation, I guaranteed them that the data gathered from the classroom observations would not be used for evaluation nor would it be seen on an individual basis by administration. Their data was their own. We would aggregate it at the grade, school, and district levels to drive our professional development agenda and school improvement goals.

The teachers called it iCollaborate because the observation data led to collaborative inquiry and discussions in staff meetings. Trained and vetted data coaches would go into a classroom for a full day and look at the child's experience during that day—time spent in whole group and small group, with a specific teaching approach, in transition, in curricular content areas, in lunch, in learning centers. Every percentage point of time equaled 4 minutes of the student's day. If 30 percent of their day was spent in whole group instruction, that was 120 minutes of whole group instruction, or 2 hours. Questions we asked: Is it developmentally appropriate for a first grader to spend that much time in whole group instruction? Should we reduce whole group and increase small group time? Should we use learning centers more? What about students having choice? What impact does student voice have on their achievement? How does the transition from grade to grade affect a student's engagement? If 45 percent of the day was done with didactic teaching approach (sage on the stage), in what ways would that impact student engagement?

While there were many spin-offs to this initiative, it was essential for teachers to discuss their instructional strategies with data collected by a third party, not the principal. It also provided the district with a clear idea of how to organize professional development and in what topical areas. Over 400 classrooms were observed and eventually, we extended it to high schools with a different instrument, Classroom Assessment Scoring System (CLASS), developed by Robert Pianta at the University of Virginia.

What happens in the classroom must be a central focus for any school leader. How you go about finding this out depends entirely upon the trust you develop with your staff and the knowledge you have as an educator to be able to speak to instruction with proficiency and authenticity.

What Does it Mean?

After analyzing the current context, asking good questions, and gathering data, the next question for Reflection is, "What does it mean?" Keep in mind that data can be collected from a wide variety of sources—verbal, textual, and nonverbal (like body language or images). Patterns can emerge from the data that will help identify your leadership goals and strategies. Here are questions you might ask as you look for patterns and sort out their meaning:

- Is there a history of student or teacher attendance that contributes to the overall school/district culture and identity?
- Does the discipline data indicate an imbalance in referrals as it relates to the demographics of the school/district culture and identity?
- What can you learn from parent/community engagement data?
- When you look out at your staff, where do you see some staff more engaged than others?
- Does your budget tell you that there are expenditures not related to students?
- Are resources allocated to the areas identified most in need in an equitable manner?

The point is that it all means something! Finding shortcuts around dedicating time to reflection will not help establish a solid foundation for your leadership. How will you know what to do in the first 100 days? Which areas could be quick wins and which will need more massaging? Is there an easy correlation between your leadership style and the areas that need addressing?

Let's take a look at a few images. Think about what these images tell you and the questions you will want to ask to clarify your perception.

A Staff Meeting

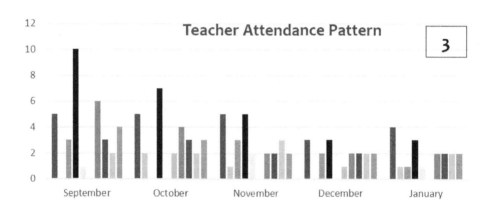

Teacher Attendance Pattern

■ Teacher 1 ■ Teacher 2 ■ Teacher 3 ■ Teacher 4 ■ Teacher 5
■ Teacher 6 ■ Teacher 7 ■ Teacher 8 ■ Teacher 9 ■ Teacher 10

Student Proficiency

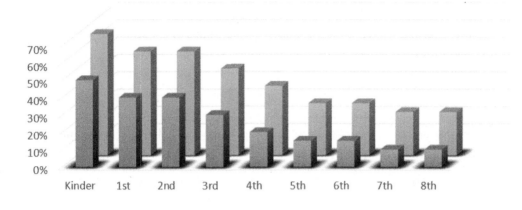

■ Math Proficiency   ■ Literacy Proficiency

Resource Allocation

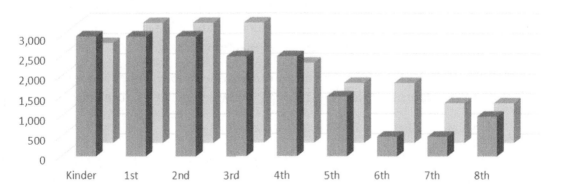

■ Math Allocation   ■ Literacy Allocation

As you look at each of these images, you likely have several observations. Let's imagine some of them:

1. Staff Meeting: Has the meeting started? Who is leading the meeting? What time of the day is the meeting being held? What's on the agenda? How do I bring everyone together to make this time productive?

2. Thanksgiving Poster: Does this represent the values of our school/district community? Is it historically representative? Is this all there was to Thanksgiving? Is there a different way to celebrate this holiday?

3. Teacher Attendance: Is there an absentee problem? What is happening in the life of Teacher #4? How is this affecting student achievement? Is there a morale problem? Which month(s) seem to be the most difficult concerning attendance? Why are they?

4. Compare A and B.

    A. Student Proficiency: Which grade levels are the highest achieving? To what do you attribute the decline in proficiency the higher the grade level? Is there a staffing or instructional quality gap between grade levels? Have the teachers administered forward and backward curricular mapping?

    B. Resource Allocation: Is the allocation equitable? Is it correlated with identified need? Is it equitable to allocate more funds to a grade level that is performing well than to one that is not performing well? How do we decide on how math and literacy funds are allocated?

Once you get accustomed to looking around you for clues that tell the story about the organizational environment and what is valued, you will be able to walk into any setting and quickly get a sense of what's happening here. From that analysis, you will better understand what it does mean and develop your plan of action—reflection—action (praxis)!

Being a reflective leader means getting out of your echo chamber and seeing the world—yourself included—through a new set of lenses. It means:

- Knowing yourself better than you may want to
- Knowing why you are where you are
- Asking why we do things the way we do them
- Analyzing for meaning

Once you start to feel your stride in your new role as a leader, reflection will be as integrated into your life as getting up in the morning and getting dressed—by the way, you can reflect while you're doing that, too!

A wonderful quote from Anaïs Nin says, "We don't see things as they are, we see them as we are." Leaders need to be able to view the world from a wide variety of angles because they are serving multiple constituencies with unique interests and cultural expressions. If the leader only sees things as s/he is, there will be very few followers—perhaps only her/himself.

Quotes that Inspire Leaders

Choose a quote that represents a quality that you feel is important in a leader or that reflects your personal philosophy of leadership, write about it, and/or share it with a colleague.

Write the quote and display it in a prominent place that will remind you of this perspective. Use as a tagline in your email signature.

Reflection:

- Attitude determines altitude. *Dr. Gary Phillips*
- Sinawa (the Great Spirit) gave us two ears and one mouth in order that we might listen twice as much as we talk. *Native American Saying*
- There are two ways of spreading light: to be the candle or the mirror that reflects it. *Edith Wharton*
- Owning our story and loving ourselves through that process is the bravest thing we'll ever do. *Dr. Brené Brown*
- What you think, you become. *Buddha*
- He who learns but does not think is lost. He who thinks but does not learn is in great danger. *Eleanor Roosevelt*
- It is better to ask some of the questions than to know all the answers. *James Thurber*
- Fall seven times, stand up eight. *Japanese Proverb*
- Great leaders don't set out to be a leader…they set out to make a difference. It's never about the role–always about the goal. *Anonymous*
- We do not learn from experience…we learn from reflecting on experience. *John Dewey*
- A good leader takes a little more than his share of the blame, a little less than his share of the credit. *Arnold Glasow*
- He who has a "why" to live for can bear almost any "how." *Friedrich Nietzsche*
- Learning without thought is labor lost. *Confucius*
- I ain't what I ought to be and I ain't what I'm going to be, but, I ain't what I was. *Anonymous*

Reflection

ACTIVITIES

KEY TO ACTIVITIES AND JOURNAL

VIGNETTE

LEADER ONLY

STAFF/TEAM

Introduction to Activities

Each chapter has a series of activities for the reader to use in her/his work as a current or aspiring leader. They address the concepts and ideas presented in the chapter and assist the leader in a deeper understanding through practice.

It is important to carefully read each one of them and reflect upon their use, with whom, when, and for what purpose. Some of the activities, especially in Chapter One, are meant for the reader/leader only as a way to journal thoughts and insights about her/his leadership. Those activities are marked with a single lock. Others, in Chapters Two and Three, are meant for both the reader/leader and her/his staff or team. Those activities are marked with two locks. If the activity is a survey, a blank survey is provided for the purpose of making copies and distributing to the participants. There is an activity at the end of each chapter that asks you to consider and journal about the many vignettes (stories) that illustrate the ideas presented in that chapter.

At the end of the book there are Growth Plans for the leader and, if desired, the staff. The plans are tied to the Activities in each chapter. Information generated from the Activities can be used to populate the Growth Plans. The leader as "scribe," can use these Growth Plans to stimulate conversation with the staff, gather evidence to improve school culture, and/or for her/his own development.

There are three surveys on Cultural Competencies that can provide unique insight to the reader/leader on the extent to which s/he and her/his staff possess the necessary elements for cultural competency. The conversations that can emerge from the analysis of the responses can be very enlightening, instructive, and, unfortunately, uncomfortable at times. The reader/leader should be very careful and intentional about using these surveys with staff or her/his team as they require a significant amount of trust for a meaningful debrief. Since I developed all of the surveys and have done many years of work on cultural awareness, I would be happy to assist the reader/leader in thinking through their use. I can provide another layer of cultural competency called "cultural revisioning," not included in this book, which speaks to what we do after we discover our cultural perspective. It's based on work by famed Dr. Peggy McIntosh and lays out five levels of cultural revisioning from ethnocentric to *symbiotic* and includes insight on Geert Hofstede's research on cultural norming (2005). You can contact me at ycaamalcanul@aol.com for more information on how I can support your work to develop a more culturally symbiotic educational environment.

Reflection Activity 1: Leadership for All Seasons

Look at each season carefully. Which one seems to resonate with your leadership style?

Summer

Action: "Let's do it!" Likes to move forward, try things, and plunge in.

Spring

Deliberating: Likes to look at the big picture and the possibilities before acting.

Winter

Compassionate: Likes to know that everyone's feelings have been taken into consideration and that their voices have been heard before acting.

Fall

Meticulous: Likes to know who, what, when, where, and why before acting.

- What are three words that describe the strengths of your season?
- What are three words that describe the limitations/challenges of your season?
- What style would/do you find most difficult to work with and why?
- In what ways can you cope with conflict with someone from another season?
- What do people from the other seasons need to know about you so you can work together effectively?
- What do you value about the other three seasons?
- What is the best combination for a group to have? Does it matter?
- How does this affect your leadership vision?

Leadership for All Seasons—Reflection Journal

Three words that describe the strengths of my season:

1.

2.

3.

Three words that describe the limitations/challenges of my season:

1.

2.

3.

The style I find most difficult to work with is:

People from the other seasons know that I am:

I value the other seasons in these ways:

Ways in which I handle conflict with another season:

The best combination for a group to have is:

Ways in which this knowledge will affect my leadership:

Typology Inventories That Are Helpful

- Myers Briggs Type Indicator–Poses a series of forced-choice self-report questions that result in a combination of four letters to indicate personality type. There are 16 personality types drawing upon the following characteristics: Introversion/Extroversion; Intuition/Sensing; Thinking/Feeling; and Judging/Perceiving. When the characteristics combine into the four-letter personality type, you have a better understanding of who you are. It can be used to identify and develop team strengths and challenges.

- Keirsey Assessments–David Keirsey and Marilyn Bates developed a typology sorter that is similar to the MBTI but has fewer questions and categorizes the types into interesting Jungian-like nomenclature: Artisans, Guardians, Idealists, and Rationals. It also looks at how typology affects childhood and parenting. Shorter version than MBTI and in a book entitled, *Please Understand Me* (1984).

- Johari Window–Provides an important insight into what you are willing to share about yourself and how others perceive you. There are four quadrants, one of which is called the "blind spot" where others perceive things about you that you do not see. The inventory is based on two important ideas–trust can be acquired by revealing information about you to others and learning about yourself from their feedback.

- Kirton Adaption-Innovation Inventory–Looks at your Creativity Style on a continuum; the left end is labeled "Adaption" and the right end, "Innovation." If you administer the KAI to your staff, there is an interesting revelation about where people fall on the continuum and helps explain how different people approach problems and solutions.

- FIRO-B–Reveals how interpersonal needs affect behavior and relationships, the result of which provides individuals with a more expanded understanding of their own behavior and the impact of other's behavior on them; what they're willing to share about themselves (expressed) and what they want from others.

- DISC–William Moulton Marston (who also wrote self-help books, developed the polygraph test, and created the character Wonder Woman!) first developed DISC theory to categorize the list of characteristics of emotions and human behavior, which he called: Dominance, Inducement, Submission, and Compliance. The actual self-assessment was first developed by Walter Clarke using Marston's model and further refined by John Geier in the 1970s to become the DISC-Profile Assessment: Dominance, Influence, Steadiness, and Conscientiousness. It is a useful tool for team building.

- Six Archetypes–Carol Pearson, in *The Hero Within* (1986), presents a fascinating journey into the personal archetypes we live by: Orphan, Wanderer, Warrior, Altruist, Innocent, and Magician. Each archetype has its own reason for being, gifts, challenges, and motivations. While it's a bit marginal to the ordinary list of typologies, it can provide a unique insight into better understanding where you are as a leader in terms of your personal development and maturity.

Typology Inventories that are Helpful—
Reflection Journal

If you have decided to find out about your typologies,
this would be a good place to record them for future reference.

- My Myers-Briggs Type Indicator (MBTI) is:

- The Keirsey Assessments indicate I am:

- My blind spot in the Johari Window is:

- Along the Kirton Adaption-Innovation Inventory continuum, I am:

- My FIRO-B indicates that I am:

- My DiSC Profile is:

- My archetype from *The Hero Within* is:

Knowing this about myself will:

Reflection Activity 2:
Self-Observation Survey

Decide on the extent to which you observe this about yourself.

Consider the following	Always	Usually	Rarely	Never
I know who I am as a person.				
I can identify the elements of my typology.				
My "why" is displayed in my workspace.				
People with whom I work know why I have chosen this profession.				
I have traveled to different countries.				
I understand and appreciate cultures that are different from mine.				
I have friends and colleagues who are critical friends.				
I think deeply about why things are as they are.				
I create and support an environment of continuous inquiry and experimentation.				
I encourage problem-solving by initiating extensive searches for contributing factors, and possible courses of action with confidence and consideration of consequences.				
Data are collected, analyzed, and used for decision-making.				
Decision-making is based on evidence, the situation, timeliness, and consequences.				
I believe that need determines allocation of resources.				

©Leader Observations. Yvonne Caamal Canul. 8.2020

Suggested Activities

- Which observations could be part of your Leader Growth Plan?

- Identify three observations to which you answered "rarely" or "never."

- Commit to make them part of your Leader Growth Plan.

Self-Observations for My Growth Plan—
Reflection Journal

Three observations to which I answered "rarely" or "never."

1.

2.

3.

Which observations do I want in my Leader Growth Plan?

Commitment Statement that will be part of my Leader Growth Plan.

Other observations I have made regarding this survey:

Reflection Activity 3: Evolution of the Leader

Look at the stages below and place a ✓ in the box to the right that most correlates to your current professional context.

Factors	Emerging	In Stride	Sundown	
Career Tenure	5–15 years	15–25 years	25+ years	
Leadership Roles	Few with some responsibility and authority; i.e., lead teacher, department chair, team lead, grant coordinator	Several with moderate responsibility and authority in a school (principal or AP) or district central office (grants/unique projects), middle management; ready for more responsibility and authority	Multiple roles, in and out of profession; re-entering after hiatus or retirement. Many roles with significant responsibility and authority	
Future Plans	Seek roles with more responsibility and authority; stay in organization	Seek district leadership; will consider move to a different organization for leadership role	Final move in profession; not interested in advancing for more responsibility and authority	
Leadership Identity	Learning more about leadership; still unsure but developing strong relationships	Clear about style; learning application of style; comfortable with role; feeling of usefulness if successful; if not, superficial engagement in role	Reflection on her/his leadership and wisdom, mentoring others if successful. Failure leads to resentment, acrimony	
Focus	Actively seeking new ideas and innovations	Integration and synthesis of new ideas and innovations	Application of ideas and developing systemic supports	
Purpose	Developing a purpose; driven to make a difference	Clear purpose; driven to excel	Sense of fulfillment and legacy	

©*Evolution of Leader. Yvonne Caamal Canul. 2020*

My Leadership Phase is: _____

Reflection Activity 4: Core Values Survey

Place a ✓ next to four of the ones by which you most want to be remembered.

☐ People can depend on me being consistent and reliable.

☐ Everyone works differently. We all know our own styles and respect each other.

☐ Knowing and respecting cultural norms is the basis for demonstrating to others that I care.

☐ I believe you should always collaborate on decision-making.

☐ Being knowledgeable is an important aspect of leadership.

☐ Everyone on my team is included and respected even when we are mad at each other.

☐ People trust me.

☐ Feelings matter. We can figure out how to deal with feelings even when they are messy.

☐ Open communication and deep inquiry are cornerstones of teamwork.

☐ Continuous learning is essential.

☐ I help those who help themselves.

☐ Getting things done is more important than stopping to smell the roses.

Note: There's another activity related to Core Values in Chapter Two on Relationships for staff to take.

Core Values Survey—Reflection Journal

Four Core Values that I most want to be remembered by and why. Where do I see evidence of these in my leadership?

1.

2.

3.

4.

Observations I have made regarding this survey:

Reflection Activity 5:
Cultural Competencies Survey

Rate these statements based on your own cultural proficiency.

Consider the following	Always	Usually	Rarely	Never
I have thought about my own racial, ethnic, gender, and social class identity and the various ways in which I am similar to or different from other groups with which I frequently interact.				
I have thought about my own racial, ethnic, gender, and social class identity and the various ways in which I am similar to or different from other groups with which I rarely, if ever, interact.				
I have thought about my own racial, ethnic, gender, and social class identity and how it influences the way I interact with others.				
I have had meaningful dialogue with colleagues and friends about cultural influences on organizational policy, politics, attitudes, program planning, learning/teaching.				
I believe my organization represents a diverse community in its mission to provide equitable access for full participation by all constituents.				
I am willing to reconsider my own cultural perspectives to effect positive change in the organization.				
I use language that is free from racial, ethnic, linguistic, physical, and sexual bias at all times.				
I believe it is acceptable to use language, stereotypic attitudes, and ethnocentric assumptions without fear of redress from colleagues.				
I frequently interact with colleagues and community members who are of different racial, ethnic, linguistic, class, spiritual, gender, or physical backgrounds.				

I attend organizational events that reflect the diversity of the organizational community.				
I have many friends who are racially, ethnically, linguistically, spiritually, and/or physically different from me.				
I regularly collect and analyze data regarding diversity issues and use it to help identify the goals and allocation of resources.				

©*Survey of Cultural Perspectives. Yvonne Caamal Canul. 2008*

Suggested Activities

- Identify three statements to which you answered "rarely" or "never."
- Which statements could be part of your Leader Growth Plan?
- Commit to make them part of your Leader Growth Plan.

Cultural Competencies for My Growth Plan

Three statements to which I answered "rarely" or "never."

1.

2.

3.

Which cultural competencies do I want to include in my Leader Growth Plan and why?

Commitment Statement that will be part of my Leader Growth Plan:

Other observations I have made regarding this survey:

Reflection Activity 6: Leader's Knowledge of Instruction Survey

Instructional strategies affect student performance and can tell us much about how learning is valued in the educational environment. School leaders should be well versed in a wide variety of strategies in order to support teacher growth. In this activity, determine the extent to which you are familiar with the strategy. In the comments section, identify five strategies you want to know more about. Use a ✓ rating from 1 (not familiar) to 5 (very familiar).

Instructional Strategy	1	2	3	4	5	Comments
Assessing prior knowledge						
Alternative assessment techniques						
Cooperative learning						
Graphic organizers/ visual tools						
Projects-based learning						
Problem-based learning						
Sheltered Instruction for ELLs						
Learning Centers						
Scientific Process lesson design						
Behavioral/Academic student contracts						
Research skills						
Manipulatives–math						
Hands-on–science, social studies						

Multiple intelligences						
Using student typology in lesson planning						
Inquiry-based discussions						
Student-led discussions and conferences						
Readers–Writers Workshop						
Thematic instruction						
Technology in the classroom						
Classroom management techniques						
Using rubrics to assess learning						
Scaffolded Instruction						
Reflective Instruction						

©*Leader's Knowledge of Instruction. Yvonne Caamal Canul. 2020*

Reflection Activity 7: Contemplating a Vignette

 In this book, a vignette is an italicized paragraph with a story that brings reality to the concepts addressed. There are several vignettes in this chapter on Reflection. As you think about each vignette, choose one that sparked a thought or insight and consider the following questions:

The vignette I have selected is about:

The reason I chose this vignette is because:

An insight I gleaned from this vignette was:

Relationships

CHAPTER 2

Relationships

INTRODUCTION

"Everyone's a potential ally, everything a potential spark." Yvonne Caamal Canul

There was a time when workshops for aspiring leaders focused on the importance of developing relationships in order to enhance and promote one's career. The strategies involved golf courses, country clubs, and after-hours socializing. While those are still activities that work for some people, access issues for many current and aspiring leaders tend to make those strategies culturally disconnected and/or financially prohibitive.

In order for any leader to become more effective, it is crucial to broaden one's definition and understanding of "relationships" as more than socialization. The importance of on-the-spot synthesizing, being able to "connect the dots" and see the relationship between ideas and data, and systems thinking—all are more important now than ever, especially in an era of information overload.

In this chapter we will explore five kinds of relationships:

- with self
- with the organization
- with others
- with/in situations
- with ideas

We will also see how these five kinds of relationships are interrelated. A leader who understands this interrelatedness can develop a broader constituency and drive a more sustainable vision. An effective leader focuses on the importance of relationships, sees, synthesizes, and makes connections. It requires keen observation, mental agility, and the ability to synthesize. In Five Minds for the Future (2007), Dr. Howard Gardner outlined essential mindsets for leadership in the twenty-first century global society: Disciplined, Synthesizing, Creating, Respectful, and Ethical. While all of the mindsets Gardner highlights are important for every leader to embody, in this chapter on relationships we will focus on the importance of being able to synthesize, "the ability to integrate ideas from different disciplines or spheres into a coherent whole and to communicate that integration to others."

This may seem a little complicated. We're not used to defining the word "relationships" as more than a me-and-you type of interaction. So, let's explore a simple example of what this expanded definition of "relationships" might look like (all five elements are hidden within the example; see if you can find them!):

You are the principal of a neighborhood school. Your students frequently stay after school hours for a variety of reasons. You also have a few staff who stay to supervise the students when school hours are over.

You have just been invited to a community function where you meet the CEO of the local YMCA. She mentions that the Y is interested in finding new ways to serve the community.

Here is where the synthesizing mind should take over and focus on the relationships this example offers. Opportunities ("dots") have just presented themselves to you:

- students staying after school
- staff who also stay after school hours
- the local YMCA is looking to expand its service

In this case, it's not enough to say, "nice to meet you" to the CEO and move on. An opportunity for a new relationship has presented itself for you to set up a meeting and explore a partnership that is consistent with the vision for your school or district.

When you connect the "opportunity dots," you now have a view of the expanded definition of Relationships where all five kinds of relationships are evident. By seizing this opportunity, you have connected your:

1. Leadership vision (with self)
2. To the school's mission (with the organization)
3. For the well-being of students and staff (with others)
4. By promoting after-school activities (with situations)
5. By supporting YMCA's expanded engagement for students (with ideas)

The relationship between all the dots has the potential for making a strong ally as well as spark an innovation for your school or district.

In the first chapter, we explored the importance of Reflection as fundamental to work in a leadership capacity. The next stage in setting the foundation for effective leadership is understanding the importance of establishing Relationships. We will focus on an expanded view of Relationships in the context of leadership because, in order to move the leader's vision forward, relationships are the key to developing a concerted community effort and true shared leadership.

Relationship with Self

"Life is like a basketball. It's all round and connected."
Betty Hale

There are five kinds of influence in *relationships*. The first is with **self.** When you become better acquainted with who you are as a leader, the relationship you have with yourself in terms of your physical, emotional, and mental well-being is essential to doing the difficult work of leading others. People are depending on you to be authentic, focused, on message, and sane! You may think the idea of sanity is a bit odd but it's really about making sure you think clearly about your reaction to things—10 percent of life is what happens to you and 90 percent is how you handle it. A friend once said that the higher up a person goes on the career ladder, the more their pathologies become apparent. There is enough drama in the world these days; no one needs yours in the workplace!

The following are important factors to help define your relationship with self:

- **Find your authentic self**—Authenticity is the core of a leadership style. No one likes to be around a fake. Remember, people are relying on you for consistency and dependability. Exhibiting a roller coaster of behaviors does not engender trust or confidence in your leadership. If you're calm and collected, people expect you to be that way most of the time. If you're animated and exuberant one day, and calm and collected the next, people will wonder what's happening with you. One of the biggest challenges a leader faces is to feel secure in her/his own skin and in the role of a leader. A charismatic leader depends on personality to move a district, but it's not sustainable. A dogmatic leader depends on authority, but eventually, people rebel. A laissez-faire leader lets people make decisions, but things start to fall apart and resort to tribalism with time. The transformational leader takes an organization to where it ought to go, but others may not agree. Some leaders attempt to hide their insecurity by plastering their office walls with certificates and awards, thereby proving competence and accomplishment. Others create warm and comfortable spaces that feel more like a living room than an office. Still others leave their workspaces relatively bare, giving the appearance of a management by walking around (MBWA) leadership style OR, it could be perceived as, "I'm not planning on being here long." Make sure your office or workspace reflects and represents you! When a person walks into your space, they should be able to see who you are. I once knew a superintendent whose wall behind her huge desk was covered with certificates and honors. That also told me a lot about the level of insecurity she had in that position.

- **Have a good sense of humor and laugh**–Some leaders believe that in order to command respect, they must be serious, officious, and stern. A good sense of humor (especially laughing at oneself) goes a long way in developing a healthy relationship with your community. Of course, making jokes at the expense of others is NOT funny. Keep in mind that humor is contextual, culturally biased, and interpretive. What may be funny to one is not to another. Play it safe and smile. The CEO of Kolt Communications, Bob Kolt, always says, "Smile with your teeth!"

- **Know who you are as a Leader**–Knowing your personal typology is one thing (Chapter One). Knowing how it influences your decision-making is quite another. Do you like to collect data/information from several sources before you make a decision? Do you ask other people their opinions before you approach an issue? Are you a "take care of business now" leader? Would you prefer to be with people and leave the paperwork for later? Would you rather do it yourself? Tom Justice and David Jamieson (1999) developed a very useful tool for decision-making, ranging from L1 (leader only) to M (absolute consensus) styles and situations. As a leader, you will face multiple decisions every day–big ones and small ones. Is your leadership style one where you alone make decisions or do you prefer consensus? It depends on the situation, the type of decision to be made, who is affected, and the time you have to make it. However, the way you approach decisions is greatly influenced by your leadership style.

- **Choose your swords carefully**–This is your "why." What is the sword you're willing to throw yourself on, the hill upon which you are willing to die? These are the issues for which there is no negotiating. Most issues can be negotiated for a win-win solution. However, some things cannot and these are generally elements of your stated values as illustrated by the following vignette.

It was not unusual for teachers to send me misbehaving students when I was a principal. One Monday, one of the teachers sent me a student who became quite upset as he arrived that morning, throwing things and yelling. When he arrived at my office, he looked exhausted, so I told him to take a seat on the couch and I'd be with him in a minute. (I had a big velvet couch in my office to make it homey.) Then I went to the teacher's classroom to find out what happened. She was angry with him and wanted him punished. As it turned out, over the weekend, she had decided to change the group seating arrangement so that the students could work with others they hadn't worked with before. Good idea. Unfortunately, she hadn't planned this change with the students nor let them know ahead of time. She also hadn't taken into account the life context of this particular student who was homeless and had been living in hotels and a car for several weeks. When he arrived, things were not where he expected them to be and it was, for him, the last straw. I let him sleep that morning and when he woke, we had a chat and he decided he could go back to class. It was not a situation that deserved punishment; it was a chance to develop trust and understanding.

For me, this was a sword worth falling on.

- **Leading with Light Leadership** is difficult and it is easy to take the low road when you feel like the world is not in your favor. There will be days when you wonder why you decided to take on such a Herculean assignment. There will be people who will try to bring you down, nip at your heels. You will need to look yourself in the mirror and dig into your own ego and power needs (very challenging). If you know why you've chosen this career, you will surround yourself with people who will tell you like it is. Continually reflect on your actions, and you can be successful. It takes a solid self-image that doesn't need to feed off others' misfortune to thrive.

Parker Palmer, author of *Let Your Life Speak: Listening for the Voice of Vocation* (1999), in an excerpt from chapter five entitled, "Leading from Within," illustrates an essential quality for leaders, especially in a time of divisiveness.

"A leader is someone with the power to project either shadow or light upon some part of the world, and upon the lives of the people who dwell there. A leader shapes the ethos in which others must live, an ethos as light-filled as heaven or as shadowy as hell. A good leader has high awareness of the interplay of inner shadow and light, lest the act of leadership do more harm than good....some shine a light that allows new growth to flourish, while others cast a shadow under which seedlings die... [in doing so] we will meet the darkness that we carry within ourselves—the ultimate source of the shadows that we project onto other people. If we do not understand that the enemy is within, we will find a thousand ways of making someone 'out there' into the enemy, becoming leaders who oppress rather than liberate others." (pp. 73–94)

Your light can either squash motivation and engagement or grow your community's commitment to your vision.

Relationship with the Organization

"He who has never learned to obey cannot be a good commander." Aristotle

Your relationship with the organization in which you work is critically important for carrying your leadership vision forward. Your organization has selected you for a leadership position because of specific qualities that you have demonstrated over time. These qualities are of value to the organization and your relationship with the organization has positioned you as a valuable asset to the organization.

Over the years, I have developed a formula called *Your Value to the Organization*. It's very simple and I've used it on several occasions to share with staff how I view their role in the community as well. Here it is:

Key to Formula:

Your Value to the Organization Formula $$w - c = V$$

w = Amount of Work I Do

c = Amount I Complain About the Amount of Work I Do

V = Your Value to the Organization

You are not alone in your organization. Your relationships are symbiotic. In other words, *you get what you give*. The relationship you have with the organization/school/district in which you work is one of the most important relationships you will have. For some people, that relationship lasts their entire career.

I had been a teacher, principal, and central office administrator in the same school district for almost 27 years. I had an opportunity to be a part of an innovative project from the state's department of education and left my district for that job, worked there for seven years, and then retired. I went on to do other kinds of work and five years later, I was asked to come back and be the interim superintendent of that district in the middle of the school year. Because of my long relationship with the district, I knew many people who were still there, including several board members. It felt like a wonderful homecoming. I stayed on for another eight years.

The Organization Also Evolves

If you think back to the chapter on Reflection and the Evolution of the Leader, you noted that the Evolution of the Organization is also on a continuum of development as is the leader. When you are clear about where you are situated in the evolutionary cycle of leadership development, you need to look at the organization (school or district) and analyze your fit within it. There is an activity at the end of this chapter that helps you determine where the organization is at your point in time of entry.

©YCaamalCanul 8.2020

As I look back at my career, I notice that I have either "put order to chaos" or built new structures where there were none or where existing ones were crumbling. That is my profile and I am at my best when there is a new challenge before me. As an Emerging leader, I started with smaller start-up projects that were directed by others but where I could show leadership talent. As one In Stride, I founded a new school and led a newly formed division in the state's department of education. In my Sundown leadership, I took over a troubled school district knowing that I would turn it over to others and that it was my last (full-time) career gig.

An organization in chaos likely needs a leader who is either In Stride or Sundown, since experience and gravitas are key to making things happen. An organization that is Developed/Optimized can be successfully led by an Emerging Leader or one that is In Stride. However, an organization that is Re-Forming would likely do better with a leader that is In Stride and willing to stay through the reformation. The experience an In Stride leader brings to an organization is essential to helping form and solidify the factors needed to bring that organization into one that is developed and stable.

Long-term tenure and shelf life are also important factors in determining your fit with the organization. A colleague once told me that the "board that hires you isn't the same as the one that fires you." Once again, knowing your organization and your phase in your continuum of development are crucial to being successful.

Be Connected to the Organization

It's important to understand the nature of connectivity. Nothing exists in isolation. One of my favorite sayings is from Betty Hale, former President and CEO of the Institute for Educational Leadership in Washington, D.C.: *"Life is like a basketball. It's all round and connected!"* Even if you leave an organization, make sure it's a positive departure. That relationship follows you for a long time.

"Uno nunca sabe para quien trabaja" is a saying in Spanish, which translated means, "You never know for whom you work." Remember the basketball? You may find yourself on the other side of the ball at times or across the table from someone with whom you had a falling out.

I had shared with administrators that if they wanted to apply for positions outside of the district, they should follow their dream but to remember that wherever they applied, that organization was going to call me, even if they hadn't listed me as a reference. I advised that they should tell me they were applying so that I could help them in their search. A principal in my district didn't particularly like me or the way I administered the district. She liked to do things on her own and rarely followed protocols. I had counseled her on several occasions, advising her of the tenuous nature of her position. She decided to look elsewhere. However, she didn't tell me. The day came for her interview in the new position and with a new organization, and guess who was on the interview committee? Yep, you guessed it, me!

Don't burn any bridges, because you never know when you'll have to cross them!

Organizational Professional Equity

You may think that an organizational chart is static, meaning that it won't significantly change over time. But, in a world of high-speed mobility, one day you could be on top, the next, not even near. It's important to understand the politics of your organization. Watch how people are promoted over time. Analyze the reasons why someone you think is undeserving might be given a new position with more authority or responsibility. Sadly, not all positions are awarded on merit. Sometimes, politics play a role. It could be as simple as a favor in exchange for a greater good, or as complicated as community perception.

Several years ago, I was on an interviewing committee for the position that was replacing me. There were some good candidates, most unknown; however, one of them was a former board member in the district and well-known to a significant constituency in the community. I believed the person selected should have great rapport with students. The other members of the interview team (all top-level central office administrators) believed otherwise. My candidate was not selected; the former board member was.

At the time, I could not understand why this happened. Many years later, when I became superintendent of the same district, I understood. Sometimes, it is better to have a person inside the tent with you than outside starting a fire.

Every organization needs to strike a balance in assigning staff to management/leadership positions. Balance criteria include seniority, racial equity and representation, experience, behavior, community connections, professional knowledge, and the ever-famous, personnel file. When you're in a leadership position, you need to be very thoughtful as to why you promote individuals. Your reasons need to be clear and understandable. The last thing you will want is for your staff to believe that you promote based on personal relationships over competence. If they believe that, they will become disheartened, less engaged in moving your vision forward, and may just look for greener pastures. When you distribute leadership, responsibility, and praise among your staff, you are more likely to become successful in advancing the mission.

Politics aside, there is just no getting away from working hard, offering solutions and not problems, adding value to the organization, and *minding your own business*.

 As a young professional, I aspired to be a part of a group called The Lunch Bunch. It was comprised of veteran staff in central office who got together once a month just to reconnect, have lunch, and talk about their jobs. There were maybe six or seven of them. One of them was my direct supervisor and I had shared with him that someday, I'd like to be a part of this group. That day finally came and I was invited to join them for lunch. During the conversations, I noticed that they were sharing stories about other colleagues, some of them not very endearing. I had a good story about one of the administrators so I jumped right in with my story (more like gossip). I thought I was now a significant member of this group since I could contribute on the same level. I was never invited back again.

The truth is, as you build your career, you also build professional equity. It's kind of like home equity in that you build a reserve of leadership acumen as you mature. In that example, I cashed in all my immature equity and had to start building it from the beginning!

Your value to the organization correlates to how you fit within the organization and the extent to which you are willing to adhere to the norms, values, and standards of behavior of the organization. Can you accept a decision without sabotage? Do you ask for permission first or forgiveness later? Do you denigrate the organization on social media? Do you volunteer for committee work? Can you honor confidentiality?

It is said that discretion is the better part of valor and in this context, nothing could be more true.

The superintendent called a veteran staff member to share with her that he had decided to make her the principal of a school. However, he told her to keep it confidential because he hadn't finished making all the assignments and things could always change. She was overjoyed about this new career move and, in her excitement, told several people that she was going to be the new principal of the identified school! Word travels fast and when the superintendent heard that his confidence had been broken, he called her up and told her that she was no longer going to be the principal. In fact, she never got a principal position in that district.

A long-serving former superintendent once said to me that he judged a person's leadership potential by two criteria: 1. How they accepted rejection; and, 2. How they handled alcohol.

My first administrative barbecue kickoff to the school year brought together about 100 staff who were department heads, school administrators, and central office cabinet members. The function was at my house and there was plenty of food and drink, both alcoholic and nonalcoholic. Remembering those two criteria, I watched how everyone behaved. Two administrators drank excessively, oblivious to the fact that they were in the house of the new superintendent. Within the year, one of them was let go, the other was fortunately counseled into a rehab program and turned out to be a successful school principal.

As you think about your value to the organization, imagine where you are situated along a scale of potential leadership positions—whether it's your first position of leadership or the next along a career ladder. This same former superintendent categorized his pool of future leaders in 4 categories:

- 25 percent I know, have heard of, all positive
- 25 percent of staff, I know, have heard of, with reservations
- 25 percent of staff, I have heard of, not always in a positive light
- 25 percent of staff I don't know, never heard of them, negative feedback

Are you in that top 25 percent of the organization? Your relationship with it will determine the extent to which you move forward in your career.

Organizational Politics and the 1, 2, 3 and 4, 5, 6 of Leadership

The final element of thinking about your relationship with the organization is something I call "1, 2, 3 is Management; 4, 5, 6 is Leadership." Being a good manager means that you can accomplish the 1, 2, 3 of the work by getting it done in a timely and responsible manner. You are organized, linear, and punctual, you follow all the rules, and you are reliable—all great qualities to have in any leadership position. However, "getting it done" does not always mean that all the ramifications have been thoroughly considered. The responsibility of a leader is to make sure the 1, 2, 3 has been vetted through a 4, 5, 6 political lens.

There are many questions to ask before making a 1, 2, 3 decision. For example: Who and how will anyone be affected? What precedent does it set? Can we deliver it long term? What else needs to be considered? Should we include others in the decision before we set things in motion? Will this contribute to the overall vision and identity of the organization?

Twenty-three years ago, I was fortunate to be attending a lecture given by Dr. Ricardo Bello Bolio, then Dean at the Autonomous University of the Yucatán in Mérida, México. He outlined the differences between having the technical knowledge and skills in our profession and the political acumen needed to be a great leader. I drew this chart in my notebook (still have it) while he was talking. It demonstrates that the more responsibility and authority you have as a leader, the more you will need to rely on political acumen.

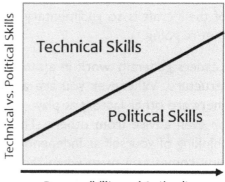

Responsibility and Authority

Dr. Howard Hickey was a wonderful professor at Michigan State University from whom I had the privilege of taking several classes. There was a great story he used to tell that, in my view, highlights this concept of technical vs. political skills:

The assembly line in the factory suddenly stops. The foreman is called to fix it, to no avail. The engineer is called to fix it. Again, nothing moves. Finally, they call the director who immediately calls the consultant. The consultant arrives, looks things over carefully, pulls out a little hammer from her briefcase and taps an area on the line three times. To everyone's surprise, the line begins to move! The director tells the consultant to send the bill. When the bill arrives, the director is shocked by the amount due. The director calls the consultant and shares the fact that it's too much for just a couple of taps and that the consultant should detail out the cost. A couple of days later, a corrected bill arrives with the following:

Total Amount Due: $1,000

Detail:

  $1.00 for the Tapping

$999.00 for Knowing Where to Tap

You will always need technical skills (the tapping) in your profession in order to be credible. However, knowing where, why, how, and who to tap, requires political skills—the 4, 5, 6. You can think of leaders who have had profound and illuminating knowledge and yet their political skills were so lacking that they enlightened only a few ardent followers. Conversely, there have been leaders with great political acumen but whose knowledge of their craft is so rudimentary that it's hard to trust they know where they're going.

Leaders generally work in a more complex organizational or community structure. Whenever you are a part of something bigger than yourself, there are other factors at play—protocols, processes, chain of command, or even advice from others. There is a certain amount of autonomy in thinking of yourself as independent of the organization; however, marginality comes at a price when the organization begins to think about your value to it.

A school that had been struggling for several years was assigned a new leadership team. The principal assigned was known for his innovation and community-building talents. During the summer before school started, he decided to gather a group of about 200 community volunteers to paint the outside of the school a rainbow of colors. He got the paint and supplies donated.

Several days later, the Chief of Operations drove by the school to check on grounds maintenance and was shocked to see the newly painted and colorful exterior from the road. Not seeing this project on the list of tasks assigned to the facilities crew, she contacted the superintendent to find out if the project had been previously approved. The superintendent had not heard of nor approved the painting project.

The principal had decided, on his own, to choose the paint colors and quality, commit volunteers to a job that had a liability potential, and didn't consider any of the work to be happening within a space larger than the school itself. He had decided to brand his school separately from the district's branding image, chose paint that wasn't code for the exterior of a school, and used people to do the work for free instead of requesting it be done or supervised by district staff hired to paint. He had addressed the 1, 2, 3 of the project but had ignored the 4, 5, 6 of the organization. In subsequent meetings with the executive team, every time his name came up, there was this legacy of rogue leadership that didn't sit well. Fortunately for him, he was a willing learner, and turned that school around. But, it would take years for him to increase his responsibility and authority, even though he had great technical knowledge of his craft.

Relationship with Others

Every relationship with others creates new opportunities. As you broaden your area of engagement, you also increase the potential for new ideas and projects which also increases your level of responsibility to these new relationships, their vision, and their agenda. It could mean the commitment to this new relationship may take time away from your core responsibilities. However, the more expansive your constituency base, the better the chances for maximizing your leadership vision. Your constituency should include members inside and outside your organization. Your colleagues are as important to your leadership future as your community. I served on several community boards because I believed this would improve the overall status of the organization I was leading. It is time consuming and difficult sometimes to say "no" to a joint project, especially if that project is not part of your vision.

You may find that this new engagement makes you see things a bit differently from what you initially planned. Sometimes, these opportunities present themselves to you; other times you must go out and get them.

For a time, I was the president of a statewide organization during which the legislature was considering defunding the programs for which this organization advocated. The president of the State Board of Education was one of the people who strongly supported defunding the programs. Being the person responsible for planning my organization's statewide conference that year, I decided to ask him to be our keynote speaker. Long shot.

Sometime later, we found ourselves together at a function, sitting at the same dinner table. Somehow, the conversation evolved to baseball. We were both big baseball fans and so the discussion began about which set of team players were the best in a given year. We went through all the lineups and for the life of us, we couldn't remember the name of the second baseman. Thinking it would eventually come to us, we moved on to other conversations. It was a very pleasant dinner. Finally, the program began and I was called to the stage to receive an award. As I walked to the stage, I remembered the name of the guy on second base! Upon reaching this new friend of mine in the hand-shaking line, I told him the name of the second baseman. He laughed and said that I was correct, with a heartier handshake.

He gave the keynote that year at the conference. The legislature continued funding the program.

Finding common ground is one of the most important things you can do in developing relationships with others. In order to find common ground, you need to have an expanded repertoire of knowledge and you need to listen to others' stories! Everyone has a story and the best way to find the common thread is to ask questions.

If we think of "potential allies," you never know how an initial partnership might evolve:

As the principal of a newly formed multilingual, multicultural school, I received a call from a colleague at Michigan State University. A recently arrived scholar from China wanted to get to know more about education in America and do a bit of research in a local school. Would I be interested in hosting the scholar at our school? I did think about the fact that we had just opened, and were not quite smoothly operational, but it would be an interesting setting for research. I checked with the chain of command for permission and once granted, I said, "You bet!" The scholar spent many wonderful days in our school, in conversation with the staff and me and eventually finalized his research with the university.

That was in 1995 and now, 25 years later, the scholar, Dr. Yong Zhao is still my friend. He has become an internationally renowned cutting-edge scholar and authority on the education enterprise, authored multiple books, and is a highly sought speaker. Even so, throughout the years, no matter where he or I have been, we have connected. You just never know what will develop from a potential ally.

That is why it's important to expand your constituency for the long-term sustainability of your leadership.

- How expansive is your constituency base?
- Does it include a diversity of people, groups, and organizations?
- Is it congruent with your mission?

One of the ways in which you can determine the extent to which you are developing expanded relationships with others is to connect the dots, each dot representing a person, group, or organization with whom you are in contact or partnership.

- Does it look like a triangle or an intricate web?
- What is your relationship with colleagues within your organization?
- Do they call upon you for advice, expertise, and counsel?
- Are you selected to local, regional, or statewide boards and/or offices?

Developing a Team of Others

Since relationships are key to moving a vision forward, no leader can do it alone. You need a team of people who are committed to your leadership vision. The way you lead and manage your team is as important as the way you lead your learning community. It takes time, knowledge of the organizational context, understanding of what needs to be done and when, and the talent pool at the leader's reach.

The leader also needs to understand how well team members work in a team setting. Some leaders prefer to lead by asking trusted colleagues to accomplish a task; others go to the acknowledged expert on staff; still others know exactly who would be the best for a task/project, and that the assignment could serve to motivate and inspire that person.

Several years ago, Robert Blake and Jane Mouton (1985) published a managerial grid based on two behavioral dimensions, from glad-handing to taskmaster. According to Blake and Mouton, each leader must find a healthy balance between:

- Concern for People: the extent to which a leader considers peoples› needs, interests, and areas of personal development when deciding how best to accomplish a task.
- Concern for Results: the extent to which a leader emphasizes concrete objectives, organizational efficiency, and productivity when deciding how best to accomplish a task.

Naturally, leaders need to focus on developing a team that can get things done while taking into account team members' talents and interests. In the long run, you won't get much done if you aren't invested in their aspirations. It is crucial to give your team members a chance to play to their strengths. Knowing your team well requires many hours of investment on the part of the leader.

My executive team (ET) met every Thursday morning from 9:00 a.m. to whenever we were done with the agenda or some emergency dictated the end. Each member had an opportunity to report information s/he thought was germane to the conversation and decision-making. Sometimes this could take several minutes, while other team members might not bring anything at all. I would watch very carefully for five things: 1. What they thought was germane (level of granularity for the work they were doing); 2. How precise they were with their presentation to the group (respect for others' time); 3. How comfortable they were with presenting the content for which they were responsible; 4. The kinds of questions they asked of their counterparts; and, 5. The reactions of other team members; did they ask questions, agree, make faces, ignore. At the beginning, some of them jokingly complained about how much time they spent in ET. As time went on, they understood that it was as much about building the team narrative and getting to know each other as it was about accomplishing the work.

How are you empowering your team to build their own teams, their own collective narrative? Who are the potential leaders on your team/staff? How are you providing them opportunities to exercise their leadership? How are you empowering others to carry the flag? Are you leading yourself out of leadership in an intentional and purposeful way? The team that surrounds you might be the most important "others" in your life. They are your work family and there are few things more gratifying for a leader than having a team that works hard, laughs often, and enjoys each other's company.

There is indeed a delicate balance between rushing to accomplishment and taking the time to make sure the team works well together and is generally copacetic.

What happens when things aren't copacetic? How do you handle dissonance? Mark Gerzon is a specialist in resolving conflict. His book, *Leading Through Conflict* (2006), proposes that, aside from many other skills, leaders also need to be mediators and outlines several elements essential for successful mediation. Among these are: Presence, Inquiry, and Dialogue.

Presence: I remember the FISH! Philosophy that was popular several years ago. In fact, I had one of the maxims as a ground rule for my executive team meetings: *Be There*. By being completely engaged in the here and now, with clear thinking and feeling, you can be more mindful of the elements causing the conflict. Is there anything more annoying than someone looking at text messages while you're trying to speak with them?

Inquiry: This is as much about listening as it is about questioning. In order to get to the root cause of the conflict, the leader must find out why. You've been in situations where each person digs into their side of a misunderstanding. No one asks questions, they just make statements to support their point of view. They are not hearing each other. Someone has to mediate and start from the beginning so that there is a clear understanding by all involved: the who, what, where, when, and WHY. To paraphrase Einstein, you can't solve a problem with the same thinking that created it.

Dialogue: In order to create a wider field of mutual interests and find common ground, a healthy conversation forces you to reduce attachment to a position. Dialogue is a give-and-take proposition in conversation. It is not "my soliloquy and your soliloquy." Have you ever been in a heated discussion where you think you're on a treadmill, going over the same issue time and again? Or, you say your piece and there's no acknowledgment by the other person that they have heard you?

This story will date me. Back in the day, there was a comedy duo named Cheech and Chong (Cheech Marin and Tommy Chong). They produced several comedy albums—long before TikTok and YouTube! One of their most famous skits, "Dave's Not Here," involves a guy in his apartment responding to the guy outside knocking on the door:

> *Guy Outside* Knocks
> *Inside Guy:* Who is it?
> *Outside Guy:* It's me, Dave. Open Up.
> *Inside Guy:* Who?
> *Outside Guy:* It's me, Dave. Open Up.
> *Inside Guy:* Dave?
> *Outside Guy:* Yeah, me, Dave.
> *Inside Guy:* Dave's not here.
> *Outside Guy:* No man, I'm Dave.
> *Inside Guy:* Sorry, man, Dave's not here.

There are several more minutes of this dialogue, but you get the idea. When you're not listening to each other, not hearing points of view, you're on a never-ending treadmill of rehashed issues.

Mediating is a powerful tool for the leader to use and model because you are intentionally or unintentionally mentoring others along the way of their own leadership path. As a leader, you are always setting an example. You are sharing your leadership qualities and characteristics. You are illustrating the importance of healthy relationships.

Others as Partners

It takes community engagement to move a vision forward. However, not all partnerships may be congruent with a leader's mission. Before you engage in a partnership with others, think deeply about the precedent it sets, the long- and short-term benefits of the partnership, and the unintended outcomes that may result from the partnership. For public school leaders, secular partnerships may be the safest to explore. Since there is a clear boundary between church and state, public school leaders must be very cautious when collaborating with non-secular organizations.

The principal of a large middle years school (grades 4-6) engaged in a partnership with a local religious organization that volunteered to do school yard beautification. They then offered after-school tutoring, which the principal embraced wholeheartedly; after all, his students certainly needed that extra help. Within time, they asked if they could use the auditorium on Sundays for their services. The principal thought that since the organization was giving so much to the school, why not? The principal did not check with district leadership on this decision (see relationship with the Organization).

The superintendent and Board of Education received several letters from community and neighborhood members sharing their concern about the permission that had been granted to a religious organization to use public property for their Sunday services. The congregation was known for their anti-LGBTQ views. This seemingly innocent partnership was now a firestorm that was suddenly revealed to the district's leadership.

From that point on, it was a very delicate dance between religious representatives and the district. The principal had not thought about the potential for unintended consequences.

A school and/or school district can partner with multiple community-based organizations. It just takes a little ingenuity, understanding that not all learning happens within the walls of a classroom, opening school doors before or after instructional hours, and believing that working collaboratively with others yields the greatest benefit for students.

There weren't enough certified art and music teachers in the district to reach every classroom on a regular but infrequent basis. However, there was an Arts Council in the community and a wonderful partnership with them developed. Local artists and musicians that were members of their association would co-locate in a school as an "Artist in Residence." They would work with students on a more frequent basis. They would also meet with classroom teachers as well as district art and music teachers for planning lessons, activities, and events. The students had a chance to be with working artists and musicians and were encouraged to express themselves through art and music. This elevated their self-esteem and gave them a broadened view of what their community had to offer. The artists had an opportunity to share their expertise and talent with students thereby creating a generation of future artists and musicians.

Many community organizations want to be engaged with schools and school districts and there are several ways in which that can happen.

Vendors as Partners

Much has been said about privatizing education services. Many favor it in order to reduce legacy costs, others are against it because it reduces union engagement. Entering into agreements with private companies to perform the operational duties can be of great benefit **IF** the partners are truly committed to the welfare of the school or district rather than always to the bottom line: profit. Funding for schools has not increased enough over the past several years to compensate for the high cost of operations such as custodial, transportation, food services, and security. Many school districts have chosen to engage with the private sector to handle the work of maintaining a brick-and-mortar infrastructure. Depending on the community, this move can cause a backlash of opposition. A school district might be one of the largest employers in the region. There is a long tradition of community members working in and for school districts.

Of course, the decision to enter into a partnership with a company/vendor is not solely the decision of the leader as these decisions are generally made at the board of education level. It's up to the leader to suggest it, make sure to present the idea in a way that illustrates the pros and cons, and understand full well that timing is everything.

During my tenure as superintendent, we privatized three operations: transportation, food and facilities management, and employee benefits. The process was a great learning experience and what I ultimately understood was that a potential partner has to know the district, community, and their business in order to make it work.

When I became superintendent in Lansing, the food services contract that my predecessors had signed was about to expire. It was time to find a new provider. One of the board members, Shirley Rodgers (who I adored, even though she was sharp-tongued at times), wanted the district to do a full search for a new provider. So, we put out a Request for Proposal (RFP). At the time, I knew very little about food services providers, but I was determined to hire a company that wanted to be a partner, not a vendor. Several companies responded; among them were the district's current provider and a company named SodexoMAGIC.

Lansing is famous for many things. It's the capital of Michigan, huge automotive manufacturing center, home of the world's largest anthrax vaccine maker, national headquarters for three prominent insurance companies, birthplace of famous authors, actors, architects, and athletes—among them, Earvin "Magic" Johnson whose mom, dad, and siblings live in Lansing and are well regarded in the community. I was stunned to discover that the district had not already embraced this incredible hometown hero in ways that would not only benefit the district but give the community a big morale boost. Here was a chance to do just that (he's the MAGIC in Sodexo). Our new partner was someone who came from our community, attended and graduated from our schools, maintained contact with his lifelong friends, and who could bring an expanded worldview for our students. The proposal submitted by SodexoMAGIC was by far the best because they knew our community well and wanted to be our partner, not just a vendor.

And what a great partner Magic has turned out to be. Aside from just being a wonderful human being, his generosity has made a huge difference in the lives of our students. He spearheaded the Thanksgiving Holiday Hope initiative, marshalled his friends to donate well over $1.5 million to the Promise Scholarship Fund, and donated memorabilia for gifts to deserving students. One evening, he brought Earth, Wind, and Fire to do a benefit concert! SodexoMAGIC has been a terrific partner as well. They are responsive to students' requests, friendly, cost-effective, and give generously to the scholarship fund.

I tell you this story for two reasons:

1. Reach out to alumni who have become successful and ask them to partner with you in supporting the school or district. You'd be surprised at how many school and district leaders choose to ignore them when a simple ask might get them on board.

2. Choose your partners wisely and with purpose. While it might be nice, it's not enough to have a famous person as a partner and it's also not enough to do business with a vendor just because of history.

Parents as Partners

Perhaps the most important partnership you can develop as a school/district leader is with the families of your students. They truly are great resources for moving your leadership vision forward. A key concept to remember is that parents are also adults who have personalities, needs, talents, and unique insights. Many school leaders only see a "parent" through the eyes of their children—they're related to the student but don't have any special place in the life of the school, outside of the PTA, raising funds, or baking cupcakes. While those activities are still important, there is so much more that partnerships with parents can offer the school community!

As a principal, I did a couple of things that changed the level of engagement with the families of the students in the school:

1. Instead of a PTA or PTO where officers are elected and where not all parents feel they have a voice in that hierarchy, I formed a Parent Advisory Council. We met each month and they generated the agenda; I listened, took notes, and developed committees around the projects. I suggested topics as well and from that council, we produced several wonderful artifacts–an Anthology of Family Holiday Traditions; A Handbook of Family Cures, Sayings, and Recipes; and Stories from our Families. Students provided artwork. These booklets were placed in the school library and we sent them to all of the other schools in the district as well as to district and city leadership. Many of the parents were not proficient in English or were semi-literate, so we recorded their input and transcribed later. In a celebration, they presented their work to the school.

2. During the school year, students would go on field trips (we'll touch on this a bit more in the chapter on Rituals). We would offer these field trips for parents prior to when the students took theirs so that they would have a similar experience that would generate conversation between parents and their children. A cute story emerged from this program. Upon returning from

the Planetarium Field Trip, I asked one of the staff chaperoning the event, "So, how did the parents like the planetarium?" She clicked her tongue and said, "Well, some of them slept during the whole presentation." Of course they did! It might have been the first time in months that they could sit in a lean-back chair, in a darkened room with stars over their heads, and soft music playing! We might have missed the conversation part of the goal, but they thoroughly enjoyed the experience and were loyal forever after!

3. While this may sound a bit like heresy, I wouldn't allow parents to volunteer in the same classrooms in which their children were learning. A child has many roles ascribed to them by their families and school might be the one place where they can explore their own roles for themselves. When a parent or family member is in the classroom, that child might feel inhibited and revert to roles ascribed to her/him at home. I wanted parents to be involved in the life of the whole school so that they wouldn't be engaged for only the one year their child was in a particular classroom. I wanted them to be part of our school family for all the years. By asking them to volunteer in classrooms where their children were not assigned, they had a chance to meet other teachers and see other students. It worked for us. Of course, they could still bring treats on special occasions for their children!

4. For years I had watched lunch period in schools. The chaos and indigestion from those 40 minutes always made me wonder if there wasn't another way to approach this time. In addition, the principal was always sorting out fights or arguments after lunch for the next two hours in a he-said, she-said investigation. Given the chance, I vowed to change this. It is a bit easier to change this process in an elementary school, but I think there is a potential for secondary schools as well. As the Assistant Principal of a large high school, I dreaded the open campus hour of unsupervised lunchtime and thought there had to be another way. But, as the principal of an elementary school, we moved forward with a project called PODs. Dr. Howard Gardner's Key School had implemented this years before and we adapted it. There were four lunch periods. During each period, after eating, students would participate in one of several Projects of Discovery (POD) sections. They ranged from world language classes to dance and art. Guess who provided the content? Yes, parents, staff, and other community members! (There's more on this in the Activity section of Chapter 3 Rituals.)

As you can see, there are many ways in which to engage parents, family members, and others related to the school community. They become part of the fabric and fiber in the life of the school, not based solely on their child's classroom that year.

Relationship with/in Situations and Ideas

$\mathcal{R}$esearcher and education theorist, John Goodlad, highlighted the unique aspects of *confluence* in education—that magical burst of innovation when *people, policy, and ideas* come together to create an important new design or concept (1984). A leader's deep understanding of the power of this confluence, and how this new way of approaching solutions through the now expanded definition of relationships, might possibly be the most important aspect driving change in the educational environment.

Not all relationships are with people nor with organizations of people. Here, I am expanding the definition of relationships by including the notion of making connections between *situations* and *ideas*. The introduction to this chapter shared a simple example of seizing an opportunity when it presents itself to illustrate the interconnected nature of relationships. If you integrate the characteristics of a synthesizing mind, you will quickly see the relationship between how situations generate good ideas and vice versa! Following are three situations that presented themselves in my tenure as superintendent from which ideas emerged changing the conventional landscape. The examples illustrate how ideas and situations don't live in isolation; they are attached to each other and, over time, create new relationships and new realities if the leader can seize the moment.

Many urban school districts face the challenge of declining enrollment. Families are moving out of the city, charter schools are siphoning off students, there is little funding to upgrade brick-and-mortar facilities that are, in some cases, 100 years old. There are more classrooms than there are students to fill them. This is a story all too familiar to many superintendents. These are situations that require synthesis with new ideas.

Situation #1:

There was a time when our school district was in expansion mode, but that ended quickly. Conversations about closing one of the three high schools (a fourth had already been closed) had raged for years. Alumni gathered to protest closing their high school and board meetings were packed with emotional public speakers. The plan that had been presented to the board was to close either the school that was built in 1929 or the one built in 1943. Ironically, neither school was large enough to incorporate the student body from the other closed school; some of them would be forced to go to the third high school on the other side of town. This was a no-win situation and likely would create a mass exodus of students to neighboring school districts.

There was a middle school that was a feeder to the two high schools being considered for closing. The data indicated that its fill rate was at 55 percent. Some elementary schools also had very low student populations. A bold idea and plan emerged from this situation. The entire district was restructured into grade configurations aligned to child development stages as well as to the unique grade level interests of teachers. All 27 schools were reconfigured into Pre-K to 3rd grade (Early Years Learning to Read); 4th to 6th (Middle Years Reading to Learn); 7th to 12th grades (High School Career and College Preparation); and, a few Pre-K to 8th grades that were specialty or Magnet Schools.

Instead of closing one big high school that would sit vacant for decades and anger hundreds of alumni, we closed four elementary schools. It was much easier to sell or repurpose a small elementary school than a behemoth high school. The plan was called, "Bold Changes=Smarter Schools: Reset for Student Success!" A logo for this plan was created that was part of all communications, PowerPoints, newsletters, and website—a visual representation of the situation (Bold Changes) and the idea generated (Smarter Schools, Student Success). The plan was presented to the Board of Education in March. By August, the district was restructured, teachers placed in grade levels of their preference, transportation routes revised, furniture moved, and students enrolled in their new schools.

There was trepidation about this bold recommendation, mostly about 7th graders going to the "big house" with older students. We sectioned off the building into grade levels and provided separate busing schedules. That was the first year of the restructuring. By the second year, people were OK with the change, after which, the "bold changes" logo was shelved since the plan was now operational.

An interesting and unanticipated spin-off was that after five years of the bold change, the highest student attendance rate was among 7th and 8th graders, which previously had the lowest attendance rate. Attrition rates between 9th and 10th grades had dropped significantly and teachers were in schools that played to their age cohort preferences.

Creating a new logo to represent the relationship between the bold restructuring and the district's mission was essential in bringing our community on board with this new reality.

Situation #2:

It was time to change the district's logo (a set of leaning books) that had been in existence for more than 20 years. The world and the district had changed since the logo had been launched and it was high time for a new image. We put out an RFP to all the graphic designers in the metro area, promising a financial reward for the winning design.

The field was narrowed to five designs. The images were displayed in the district's school board meeting room for viewing and voting. A recommendation of the winning image was made to and accepted by the board. We went from the idea of leaning books to one that had the city's skyline inserted into a globe topped with a graduation cap and tassel. It was recognizable (city skyline), indicated the district's mission (graduation), and had parts that could be used in a variety of media. The previous "bold changes" logo had already been put to bed and a new district logo emerged.

When you are ready to launch a new idea and create a new reality, it's important to design a visual image that makes the idea more tangible and concrete. The relationship between an idea and the image that represents the idea creates a new identity for the organization and symbolizes what will happen because of this new identity. By repositioning the district in a different way through this visual representation, it illustrates the confluence of the expanded definition of relationships: **self**—me, as new leader with a new style; **organization**—inclusion of staff in the decision; **others**—multiple partnerships and input; **situations**—need for a new image to reflect a new reality; and, **ideas**—envisioning our new identity.

Situation #3:

Even after all the bold changes, we still had more facilities than we had students to populate them. Typically, districts would sell their vacant schools to charter schools, churches, or other not-for-profit organizations for much less than the market value. Our district had several buildings for sale. However, selling to a competitor was not prudent in an environment of highly competitive recruitment of students. The days when $1 could buy you an old school were over. In a casual conversation with the mayor at the time, I learned that the police department was looking for a new home; the lease on their precinct was owned by a private company and was about to expire.

We had a large former high school that had been built during the growing years and was used as a hodge-podge of district program offices, with a small community center and a pool in desperate need of repair. I approached the mayor with the idea of moving the city police department to this vacant former high school. The agreement was that the district would carry the cost of repairing the pool, the city would carry the cost of remodeling the site for police work, and a five-year lease would be arranged in which they would pay only utilities for the first three years while they recouped the remodeling costs. They would occupy about 85 percent of the facility, and have use of the pool, gymnasium, and auditorium. In the meantime, they would explore ways in which to build their own facility. To this day, the police department continues to occupy the facility. It was an unusual partnership, but one that has worked well over the years.

Both the district and the city had unique situations—one needed a new space, the other had too much space. The new idea was born out of the situations each entity faced.

Not all ideas generated must stay within the boundaries of a specific professional arena. A school district and the schools within the district belong to the community. Districts are stewards of the community's financial assets and can create partnerships that benefit both the community and improve the economic well-being of the district.

There are many examples in a leader's life that bring situations together with ideas and vice versa. Don't squander an opportunity to embrace those that seem uncommon. They may become your leadership's legacy and have a profound positive impact on the organization.

Quotes that Inspire Leaders

Choose a quote that represents a quality that you feel is important in a leader or that reflects your personal philosophy of leadership, write about it, and/or share it with a colleague.

Write the quote and display it in a prominent place that will remind you of this perspective. Use as a tagline in your email signature.

Relationships:

- If your actions inspire others to dream more, learn more, do more and become more, you are a leader.

- You don't inspire your teammates by showing them how amazing you are. You inspire them by showing them how amazing they are. *Robyn Benincasa*

- Leaders become great, not because of their power but because of their ability to empower others. *John Maxwell*

- You can do what I cannot do. I can do what you cannot. Together we can do great things. *Mother Teresa*

- Great leaders harness personal courage, capture the hearts and minds of others, and empower new leaders to make the world a better place. *Maxine Driscoll*

- Treat people as if they were what they ought to be and you can help them become what they are capable of becoming. *Johann Wolfgang von Goethe*

- It is better for a leader to make a mistake in forgiving than to make a mistake in punishing. *Prophet Muhammad*

- People will forget what you said, people will forget what you did, but people will never forget how you made them feel. *Maya Angelou*

- When a leader's best work is done, the people say, "We did it ourselves!" *Lao-Tzu*

- We make a living by what we get; we make a life by what we give. *Winston Churchill*

- Education is the ability to perceive the hidden connections between phenomena. *Vaclav Havel*

- In the end, we will remember not the words of our enemies, but the silence of our friends. *Martin Luther King Jr.*

CHAPTER 2

Relationships

ACTIVITIES

KEY TO ACTIVITIES AND JOURNAL

VIGNETTE

LEADER ONLY

STAFF/TEAM

Relationships Activity 1: Observations

Consider the following	Always	Usually	Rarely	Never
The people I work with know who I am as a leader.				
I lead by example, discretion, trustworthiness, and standing by my commitments.				
I am committed to lifelong learning.				
I accept responsibility for decisions made.				
I hold myself accountable.				
I foster collaborative work by involving multiple stakeholders.				
In my organization, I try to influence practice and policy.				
I have identified potential leaders and I delegate and mentor with purpose and support.				
The feedback that I provide is intentional and based on evidence.				
I value the contributions of others and frequently draw upon their expertise.				
I work with our community to identify a shared focus.				
I have developed external partnerships that are inclusive and mission-centric.				
I value all voices.				
I am committed to open, purposeful, and ongoing communication.				
I make sure several ideas are generated before we implement a program or project.				
I am comfortable in situations that challenge my perspective.				

©Leader Observations. Yvonne Caamal Canul. 8.2020

Suggested Activities

- Share your responses to these observations with your staff/team and use for discussion to take the "temperature" of your leadership.

- Give this survey to your staff/team for discussion about how to improve coherence.

- Use their answers to the inventory for your Leader Growth Plan.

Staff/Team Observations Survey— Relationships Journal

Indicate the extent to which you believe these statements are reflective of your leader's character.

Consider the Following	Always	Usually	Rarely	Never
The Leader…				
Is known by the people with whom s/he works.				
Leads by example, discretion, trustworthiness, and standing by her/his commitments.				
Is committed to lifelong learning.				
Accepts responsibility for decisions made.				
Holds her/himself accountable.				
Fosters collaborative work by involving multiple stakeholders.				
Tries to influence practice and policy in the organization.				
Has identified potential leaders, delegates, and mentors with purpose and support.				
Provides feedback that is intentional and based on evidence.				
Values the contributions of others and frequently draws upon their expertise.				
Has identified a shared focus with the community.				
Has developed external partnerships that are inclusive and mission-centric.				
Values all voices.				
Is committed to open, purposeful, and ongoing communication.				
Generates several ideas before implementing a program or project.				
Is comfortable in situations that challenge her/his perspective.				

Observations—
Relationships Journal

Three observations to which I answered "rarely" or "never."

    1.

    2.

    3.

Three observations to which I answered "always" or "usually."

    1.

    2.

    3.

What patterns or trends emerged?

After the discussion with the staff/team about how to improve coherence, we will add these three actions to our Collective Growth Plan.

    1.

    2.

    3.

Relationships Activity 2: Evolution of the Organization

Look at the stages below and place a ✓ in the box to the right that most correlates to your current organization's context.

Factors	Re/Forming		Developed/Optimized		Decline/Resigned/Chaos	
Decision-Making	Reactive, ad hoc, localized, not communicated		Based on strategic plan & data, transparent, anticipatory, designated role dependent		Individualized, hidden, personalized, communicated to a few, based on limited data, protracted/delayed	
Leadership	One leader with small team, newly formed		Organizational chart/roles well-defined, one leader with representative team		Ghost leadership, team keeps changing, no cohesion, uncertain responsibility	
Strategic Plan	No strategic plan only compliance plan		Clear, communicated, and inclusive strategic plan, displayed		Strategic plan is from years ago, on shelf	
Use of Data	Minimal data usage, mostly student achievement and attendance		Data used for decision-making, allocation of resources, multiple data sets, communicated to community		Budgetary data twice a year, some student data for evaluation of leadership	
Professional Learning	Mandatory for compliance, ad hoc		Varied training opportunities, coaches, mentoring, leadership development		Leadership and favorites go to conferences	
Protocols and Processes	Non-cohesive, changing, unclear chain of command, based on past practice		Clear chain of command, protocols and processes are communicated, cohesive across the organization, based on vision forward		Person-dependent, names of departed employees still on paperwork, no clear process, chain of command based on favoritism, constantly changing, localized/loosely coupled	

Personnel	Vague leadership structure, high turnover rate	Stable employee base, active recruitment, leadership structure is stable long-term	Exodus of employees, leadership hangs on for compensation, organizational chart is constantly changing	
Budget/ Resources	New to budgetary responsibility, resource allocation is decided by accountants and compliance office, localized, no central input or master plan	Input from users, surveys and data used for resource allocation, annual budgetary process begins early, projecting budgeting bi-monthly, centralized budgeting with stakeholders and board	Communicated to only a few, resources allocated to favorites or for compliance with funding guidelines, no input from users, emergency budgeting	

©*Evolution of Organization. Yvonne Caamal Canul. 2020*

Our Organizational Phase: _____

Relationships Activity 3:   SAMPLE
Political Skills—1, 2, 3 or 4, 5, 6

Provided in each chapter are several vignettes that illustrate the concepts presented about leadership. In this activity, you will dig a little deeper into the differences between being a manager with a 1, 2, 3 approach to decision-making and that of a leader with a broader view, the 4, 5, 6 when considering an action and/or decision.

Below is an example of how this might look in practice.

In one of the schools we worked at, staff meetings were held in the first-grade classroom located across the hall from the Principal's office. Teachers had to sit in first-grade chairs at first-grade tables during the meeting. The teacher of that classroom sat at her desk several feet away from the congregated area. The principal conducted the meeting from a first-grade chair. This classroom was also the main storage area for the school's construction paper and Kleenex.

Event, Action, or Decision	1, 2, 3 Consideration	4, 5, 6 Consideration
Scheduling the Meeting	After school	Are there times when a meeting might have more engagement from staff?
Location of the Meeting	Nearest room to the office for Principal convenience	Is there a neutral space that is large enough for all the staff? Can the meeting location rotate?
Content of the Meeting	List of operational agenda items presented to whole group by Principal	Are there important issues that need discussion? Can staff be grouped into think-pair-share setting to maximize input?
Meeting Norms	Established by the Principal	Collaboratively established with the staff.

Leading the Meeting	Principal	Are there topics on the agenda that could be led by members of the staff?
Starting the Meeting	First item on the agenda	Is there an activity that can set the tone for a positive meeting? Good things to share? A shared motivation?
Food for the Meeting	No food or drink	Is there a schedule established where staff bring treats to the meeting? Drinks provided by the Principal?
Ending the Meeting	Last item on the agenda	What is something to take away from the meeting? Is there an activity that can provide staff with a hopeful and positive perspective? Have they been appreciated?

©1,2,3 or 4,5,6 Political Skills. Yvonne Caamal Canul. 8.2020

Relationships Activity 3:
Political Skills—1, 2, 3 or 4, 5, 6

 From the many vignettes in this book, select one and analyze it from a 1, 2, 3 and 4, 5, 6 perspective as provided in the sample.

Vignette selected:

Action or Decision	1, 2, 3 Consideration	4, 5, 6 Consideration

Three decisions I make that need more of a 4, 5, 6 perspective:

1.

2.

3.

I learned that 4, 5, 6 can help me by:

Relationships Activity 4: Core Values Survey

In Chapter 1: Reflection, you identified your own core values. For a more comprehensive look at your leadership values, give the survey to your staff.

Directions for taking the survey:

- Copy the blank survey on the next page for distribution.
- Have them select three values they will remember about you years from now when they think about your leadership.
- Have them list other values they see in your leadership that are not on the inventory.

Debrief:

- In a staff/team meeting, have them share their thinking with the person next to them about your leadership as it relates to core values:
  - The values they chose evident in your leadership.
  - Discuss why they think these are important to you and how one would "see" these in your leadership.
  - How they know it's important to your leadership.
  - Why that value is important.

Relationships Activity 4: Staff/Team Core Values Survey

Select three values you will remember years from now when you think about your leader.

☐ People can depend on her/him being consistent and reliable.

☐ Everyone works differently. We all know our own styles and respect each other.

☐ Knowing and respecting cultural norms is the basis for demonstrating to others that s/he cares.

☐ S/he believes decision-making is always collaborative.

☐ Being knowledgeable is an important aspect of her/his leadership.

☐ Everyone on the team is included and respected even when we are mad at each other.

☐ People trust her/him.

☐ Feelings matter. We can figure out how to deal with feelings even when they are messy.

☐ Open communication and deep inquiry are cornerstones of teamwork.

☐ Continuous learning is essential.

☐ S/he helps those who help themselves.

☐ Getting things done is more important than stopping to smell the roses.

Core Values—Relationships Journal

Three Core Values that the staff/team most wants to remember me by and why.

   1.

   2.

   3.

Where the staff/team sees those values in action.

   1.

   2.

   3.

Observations staff/team have made regarding values they see in my leadership that are not in the inventory.

.

Relationships Activity 5: Leader Survey of Cultural Competencies—in Action

Indicate the extent to which you believe these statements are evident in your school.

Consider the following	Always	Usually	Rarely	Never
A committee reviews ways in which to integrate the entire curriculum with racial, ethnic, class, and gender content.				
We offer a program of learning that includes diversity studies.				
We provide staff with ongoing professional learning focused on diversity education and issues.				
Staff are identified to address organizational diversity concerns.				
There is a plan for integrating diversity in our routines, events, activities, and artifacts.				
We have a committee to oversee a diversity plan.				
Data are collected and analyzed regarding diversity issues and used to help identify measurable goals for plan.				
There is adequate funding and administrative support to develop, implement, and sustain the plan.				
We have policy that explicitly condemns racially, ethnically, linguistically, spiritually, gender, or physically biased behavior.				
We have clear definitions and explanations as to what constitutes racially, ethnically, linguistically, spiritually, gender, or physically biased behavior.				
Communiqués to the community are written in the language(s) of the community.				
Personnel of the organization are equitably representative of the community at each level of the organizational hierarchy.				
Consequences for violating "bias" policies are clearly stated and regularly publicized.				

©Survey of Cultural Perspectives. Yvonne Caamal Canul. 2008

Suggested Activity

- Give this survey to your staff/team for discussion about how to improve cultural proficiency.
- Share your answers to this survey with your staff and use for discussion about the extent to which your collective cultural competencies are evident in your school community. *Blank survey on the next page.*
- Use all answers for a Collective Growth Plan on page 181.

Relationships Activity 5: Staff Survey of Cultural Competencies—in Action

Indicate the extent to which you believe these statements are evident in your school.

Consider the following	Always	Usually	Rarely	Never
A committee reviews ways in which to integrate the entire curriculum with racial, ethnic, class, and gender content.				
We offer a program of learning that includes diversity studies.				
We provide staff with ongoing professional learning focused on diversity education and issues.				
Staff are identified to address organizational diversity concerns.				
There is a plan for integrating diversity in our routines, events, activities, and artifacts.				
We have a committee to oversee a diversity plan.				
Data are collected and analyzed regarding diversity issues and used to help identify measurable goals for plan.				
There is adequate funding and administrative support to develop, implement, and sustain the plan.				
We have policy that explicitly condemns racially, ethnically, linguistically, spiritually, gender, or physically biased behavior.				
We have clear definitions and explanations as to what constitutes racially, ethnically, linguistically, spiritually, gender, or physically biased behavior.				
Communiqués to the community are written in the language(s) of the community.				
Personnel of the organization are equitably representative of the community at each level of the organizational hierarchy.				
Consequences for violating "bias" policies are clearly stated and regularly publicized.				

©Survey of Cultural Perspectives. Yvonne Caamal Canul. 2008

Cultural Competencies—Relationships Journal

Three statements to which our staff/team answered "rarely" or "never."

1.

2.

3.

Three statements to which our staff/team answered "always" or "usually."

1.

2.

3.

Other observations staff/team made regarding this survey:

From the discussion with our staff/team about how to improve cultural proficiency within the school community, we will add these three actions to our Collective Growth Plan.

1.

2.

3.

Relationships Activity 6:
Partner Matrix

Here is a model of a visible way to keep your partnerships organized. You can post this somewhere prominent in the school and have one in your own set of important documents.

Partner	Activity	Schedule	Goal	Cost

©*Partner Matrix Template. Yvonne Caamal Canul. 8.2020*

Example Definitions:

☐ Partner: Name of the partner or person representing the organization with whom you have a partnership.

☐ Activity: Type of service or activity the partner provides.

☐ Schedule: When to expect the partner to provide the activity or service.

☐ Goal: How this activity or service addresses strategic goals for your student body.

☐ Cost: Resources needed to provide this activity or service.

Partnerships—Relationships Journal

Choose the three most important partnerships you have.

1.

2.

3.

Why are these partnerships important to have for your school?

What protocols in your organization were taken into consideration in developing each partnership?

What are the cost considerations?

In what ways does each partnership support your vision for student and/or community engagement?

Relationships Activity 7: Contemplating a Vignette

 In this book, a vignette is an italicized paragraph with a story that brings reality to the concepts addressed. There are several vignettes in this chapter on Relationships. As you think about each vignette, choose one that sparked a thought or insight and consider the following questions:

The vignette I have selected is about:

The reason I chose this vignette is because:

An insight I gleaned from this vignette was:

Rituals

CHAPTER 3

Rituals

INTRODUCTION

"Ritual affirms the common patterns, the values, the shared joys, risks, sorrows, and changes that bind a community together." Starhawk

If you don't think rituals have an impact on human behavior, ask baseball players what they do before every at bat! A sequence of physical foxtrots is performed as they approach the batting stance. Some never change their socks during the entire season. Others write a specific word in the dirt at home plate. In fact, the world of sports has many rituals—seventh inning stretch, half-time show, the Masters green jacket, and retiring player numbers, among others. You may think that some of these behaviors are superstitions, but they are actually a form of ritual. The belief is that if I do the same thing every time with an expectation of a specific result, that desired result will happen. More importantly for our purposes, rituals also serve to create societal bonds that can connect us to the past and shape a future narrative. They provide a consistent touch point with the here and now and create a living short story for you and/or your family. Rituals are the weft and warp of a society's culture.

Rituals can take different forms. In this chapter, we will explore them in the context of:

- Meaningful Routines
- Events
- Activities
- Artifacts

Think about your own daily rituals and meaningful routines. Do they involve a morning cup of coffee or tea? A quick check of your phone for email or texts? A moment for mindfulness before you head out the door? Packing a lunch for the kids? What happens when that "ritual" doesn't happen? Things just seem a little off-kilter. The day might be like getting up on the wrong side of the bed—the fact that there is a wrong side is also part of ritual thinking, originating in Roman times when the belief was that it was bad luck to begin the day on your left foot!

Psychiatrist Dr. Abigail Brenner wrote that rituals, "give our lives a sense of purpose and meaning, a sense of belonging, and a sense of consistent structure that can provide stability in an unpredictable world" (2015). For an individual, the hope for certainty and stability makes rituals a part of a life's meaningful routines.

However, not all rituals are for individual grounding or a desired future result. A ritual can also help create and establish a group or community narrative and the expectations for participation in that community. The narratives make history, bind the community into a shared vision, and assist the leader in establishing and sustaining the core mission of the group. Rituals are foundational in creating school culture, a school personality. They help establish the underlying norms and values that shape the behaviors and attitudes of the school community's stakeholders. As Deal and Peterson (2009) say, school culture is defined by "norms, values, beliefs, traditions, and rituals built up over time."

Do schools have rituals? There are likely more rituals in schools than in any other public institution in the world: graduation, Pledge of Allegiance, roll call, bells between classes, mascot logos, school song, holiday celebrations, and many more! The purpose of these rituals is to create cohesive community expectations and narrative; something that binds people together as one: a nation as one, a congregation as one, a school as one, a family as one. While rituals establish a firm grip on the past and present, they can also provide the structure for a desired future, transforming current reality. Transmitted by stakeholders, rituals define the school culture more vividly and act as the glue that binds the stakeholders to a shared purpose, shared belonging, and sense of identity.

The transmission of school culture through rituals happens at three different levels of explicitness (there is a chart on page 118 that illustrates these levels):

- Formal
- Non-Formal
- Informal

In this chapter, we will take a closer look at how rituals are manifested and transmitted and how they can form a school's culture. We will spend a bit of time defining school culture since that is the overarching result of implementing rituals. Leaders need to be decisively aware of the importance of rituals in framing school culture since they are all part of what constitutes a school's culture. Whether they are explicit or implicit, a school's cultural environment is comprised of meaningful routines, events, activities, and artifacts. They are all a form of ritual and are foundational to creating a consistent structure in order to provide to stakeholders a real sense of belonging, meaning, purpose, and encouragement to participate fully in their desired results. Rituals can bind the community into a shared vision as well as assist the leader in establishing and sustaining the group's core mission.

Questions you might consider as a new leader are: How do I get my new school community/staff to move in the direction I envision? How do I change or reinforce the school's culture? What do I need to put in place to make concrete a shared sense of identity? We've already explored the importance of Reflection and Relationships (and if you're asking the question of how to engage your staff, then you are squarely in a reflection mode!).

It's time to make tangible your envisioned future.

Let's dig a little deeper into the third "R" of Leadership: Rituals.

Rituals

"We are what we repeatedly do. Excellence then is not an act, but a habit."   Will Durant

"Without expressive events, any culture will die. In the absence of ceremony or ritual, important values have no impact." (Deal and Kennedy 2000)

When you hear the word "ritual," you might think of it referring to an event that has spiritual meaning. In fact, rituals can have spiritual meaning, but in this context, a ritual is a habitual event that is a predictable part of an organization's or group's culture. Every institution has a set of rituals, meaningful routines, events, activities, and artifacts that create and make tangible the narrative and identity of that institution and for each individual within it.

Note: In this chapter, we depart from the structure of the previous two chapters. We will spend more time exploring the definition of rituals, the symbiotic relationship between rituals and culture, and the unique elements that shape culture before delving into each subcategory of rituals mentioned in the introduction.

Rituals—Meaning and Manifestation

Before we examine the specifics of how rituals help establish an organizational or school culture, we need to unpack the whole notion of rituals in our society and in schooling. Let's begin with a working definition: *A ritual is something we do that we believe will yield a desired result.* Many professional athletes and entertainers have a series of rituals they go through before every performance. The expectation is that the ritual will bring about a desired and positive result. There might be science to support the notion:

> "Recently, a series of investigations by psychologists have (sic.) revealed intriguing new results demonstrating that rituals can have a causal impact on people's thoughts, feelings, and behaviors... Because people believe that, 'performing rituals with the intention of producing a certain result appears to be sufficient for that result to come true.'" (Gino and Norton 2013)

Symbols and artifacts are also used in a *ritualized* way to yield a desired result. Many people have "lucky" ties, charm bracelets, amulets, crystals, colors. We know of *feng shui*, hanging horseshoes upside down, or having a water fountain in a room. These embody the hope for a desired goal, whether it's a new job, a home run, safe travel, health, love, calm, or a change in attitude.

Rituals We Know and Practice

Below are examples of a few well-known rituals:

- "Take Me Out to the Ball Game" (written in 1908) is a ritual that is practiced at Chicago Cubs home games in the seventh inning stretch, sung by celebrities
- Blowing out the candles on a birthday cake
- Skaters go counterclockwise in skating rinks
- High-five a colleague for a positive/happy event
- Shaking hands upon meeting (now fist or elbow bump as a pandemic alternative)
- Costumes on Halloween
- Love letters on Valentine's Day
- Green beer on St. Patrick's Day
- Knock on wood to ward off calamity
- Bless you for sneezing
- Milk and cookies for Santa
- Holding the door open for someone
- Jumping the Broom
- Business owner saves the first dollar earned and posts it on the wall
- Giving a wallet as a gift, you put money in it
- Graduation open house
- Quinceañera
- Bride opens gift, breaks the bow indicating she will have a child
- Tossing the bouquet at wedding
- Carving pumpkins
- Kissing under the mistletoe
- Find a penny as good luck

Rituals come in many different shapes and sizes! Institutions are well known for their rituals, rites of passage, identity images, celebratory events, and tangible artifacts. They exist essentially to help establish and maintain the community narrative and historical placement. One of the ways in which you solidify your stability as an institution is by concretizing the culture of the institution through rituals. They memorialize the institution and make it part of the fabric of the community. Of course, there are many, many more than the ones listed above. Think of some you know. As an activity, ask your staff to list ones they acknowledge in school, in their lives, or in their community.

Rituals in Schooling

Public Education is an institution and schools are the living embodiment of the institution. How do you bring together hundreds of children into one place without implementing a myriad of rituals to get desired results and develop a collective narrative? It would be chaos if there wasn't a strong thread of group understanding with regard to behavior, values, and norms plus the rituals that maintain the collective narrative.

In fact, the public school system was designed to do just that. In the early twentieth century, the population was exploding because of the Industrial Revolution. Immigration from Europe, especially around the Mediterranean, was high with hundreds arriving daily to Ellis Island; 1.3 million in 1907 alone. None of them spoke English, most had no formal education and were agrarian. They came as laborers to work in the factories, as masons to build the new structures, and as servants to support the growing elite. The United States needed people who understood how to work in a new non-agrarian way and who could communicate in English. About this time, the Progressive Era for education in the United States pushed for building more schools, especially in metropolitan areas. Schooling became a solution for three problems: enculturation of new immigrants; childcare; and developing the next generation labor force. *E pluribus unum*—Out of many, one.

The Pledge of Allegiance is one of the most enduring ways that rituals are manifested in schools. Originally created in 1887 by the auditor of the New York Board of Education, George Balch, it once read: *We give our heads and hearts to God and our country; one country, one language, one flag!* This version was widely used in schools across the country. In 1957 it was changed to the current pledge and continues to play a significant role as a ritual to safeguard national loyalty and identity.

If you look at schools today, you can still see other vestiges of the rituals designed to help the immigrant become enculturated into the industrial work environment: start and end times, bells in specific units of time, seat time for credit, and an "assembly line" of learning content. This is especially true in high schools where a student might see six different teachers thereby "assembling knowledge." While many schools are trying to move away from this now antiquated system, cultural and historic traditions take time to change. Speeding up the change, however, is the rush of new technology. These technologies have a huge impetus for reforming the way we organize schooling, especially now that we are facing a major crossroads with regard to changing the way we view schooling, outside of a brick-and-mortar classroom.

Rituals Create Culture

As we have already mentioned, culture is comprised of and often visibly represented by its rituals: routines, activities, events, images, artifacts, language and lexicon, ceremonies, and expressed or assumed behaviors. The founder of cultural anthropology, Edward Burnett Tylor, defined culture in 1871 as "that complex whole which includes knowledge, beliefs, art, law, morals, customs and any other capabilities and habits acquired by a member of society." Culture is about being in a group, with a shared narrative, with patterns of behavior and expectations. Rituals make these expectations predictable, consistent, and universally performed.

Not all rituals are beneficial to creating and maintaining a healthy culture. Whenever groups come together, they create a culture and come to it with very different values, morals, customs, expectations, and rituals. The American school system was meant to be the great "homogenizer" and has been reasonably successful in bringing together a nation of many. However, it is not an easy process and takes time and attention. A school's culture can become quite toxic if the elements of that culture (rituals through expressed and assumed behaviors, expectations, etc.) are not addressed.

Ever since "A Nation at Risk" was published in 1983, there have been multiple initiatives in education to "fix" schools. One could argue the merits of the report, but public sentiment favored more accountability. The notion was that if we just made people more accountable, things would improve. The question is how do you make people more accountable and in what ways? Longer school days? More school days? A set curriculum? Standardized tests? My father was an educator and used to say, "Don't tell me you've been teaching for 29 years. You could be teaching the first year over 28 times." The point is that increasing time without changing what happens during that time will not fix anything. A set curriculum taught in an ineffective way will not increase student performance.

In order to help "fix" anything, you first have to find out what makes it tick (or not tick). For schools, you need to unpack the rituals of the school to find out how their culture is manifested—do they have meaningful routines, are there events for all stakeholders, are their activities representative of the community, do the artifacts illustrate their desired identity? All of these elements have a lasting impact on the success of a school because it creates the kind of environment in which there is either nurturing or discouragement, action or apathy, fulfillment or frustration. It's how people—students and staff—live every day. Imagine what it would be like in your own home if the environment was harmful. Just stepping through your front door could make your anxiety level rise.

However, you can't just walk into a school and make immediate conclusions about its culture without having a plan of inquiry and analysis in place. Several years ago when I was responsible for launching a statewide school reform program in which veteran educators would work in "priority" (underperforming) schools, the model we used for unpacking the many aspects of a school's culture was from the consultation and coaching work of Dr. Edgar Schein. (*Process Consultation*, 1988) Dr. Schein, Professor Emeritus of the Massachusetts Institute of Technology Sloan School of Management, is recognized for his work in organizational culture. The core of Schein's consultation model, simply put, is to ask good questions. The veteran educators were trained to look deeply at school culture in order to identify the key factors behind lackluster performance by using Schein's levels of school culture to guide the inquiry: (Schein. 2017)

- Take a look at the Artifacts since they represent the visible aspects of school culture
  - Ask people about them, their meaning
- Ask questions about Stated Values and Underlying Assumptions because they are what reflect shared ideas on how things should be, and what people believe, perceive, and feel
  - Ask people <u>why</u> things are done the way they are
  - Ask people <u>how</u> these things are implemented

Leaders need to do the same kind of analysis in order to better understand the context of their school/district culture and approach reform with thoughtful consideration. Keep in mind that,

> "Organizations do not adopt a culture in a single day, instead it is formed in due course of time as the employees go through various changes, adapt to the external environment and solve problems. They gain from their past experiences and start practicing it every day thus forming the culture of the workplace. The new employees also strive hard to adjust to the new culture and enjoy a stress-free life." (Sonia Krukeja. Edgar Schein's Model of Organization Culture. Article in Management Study HQ.)

Ritual as Transmission of Culture

In the work I have done around cultural competencies, I have learned that culture is transmitted through its rituals in three primary ways—at the Formal, Non-Formal, and Informal levels of action. The following table illustrates the ways in which culture is transmitted and the aspects of that transmission. For example: How do you know that the fork goes on the left side of the place setting and the knife and spoon on the right? How do you know that laughing too loud in some places is unacceptable but in others is perfectly fine? How do you know the words to your alma mater's hymn? This knowledge is transmitted through Informal, Non-Formal, and Formal enculturation.

Framework	Primary Function	Method of Transmission	Content of Transmission
Formal	Visible and tangible, images, symbols, decoration, written	Transmission is through written, visual images, symbols, songs, sayings, mottos, logos, clothing, signs; more static in nature	Content is formally recognized in handbooks, posters, plaques, statues, certificates, dress codes
Non-Formal	Embedded rules, protocols, processes, stated values	Transmission is horizontal & organic; group "think" comments about acceptable behavior, the way things are done around here, what we think about students, work schedule (not posted but practiced); more dynamic in nature	Short-term for the moment such as a meeting time, agenda, and behavior (raising hands to speak) work hours not posted, side comments, helpful "hints" from others
Informal	Ongoing, covert, "socialization" of cultural norms, values, standards of behavior, basic assumptions	Transmission is generational, through nuclear/extended families, friends, and adult/peer modeling; in schools transmission is through rituals, standards of behavior	Norms, standards of behavior-distance, voice, tone, gesture, age & gender interaction; power, position, authority; etiquette based on class; rituals, rites of passage

Many elements of culture, especially rituals, are explicit at the formal level of transmission. However, some rituals, as well as norms and values, are much harder to decipher at the informal and non-formal levels. As Edward Hall (1959) would remind us, "Culture controls our behavior in <u>deep and persisting ways</u>—many of which are outside of our own awareness and therefore beyond the conscious control of the individual."

While some behaviors might be outside one's own awareness, there are people who will remind you.

My hair is shoulder length, blondish with bangs. It's rarely styled, just clean and combed. One day I received a handwritten 3x5 postcard from an "Anonymous Tax Payer" admonishing me for having hair that was inappropriate for the position I had as a superintendent. I thought long and hard about what would be an appropriate hairstyle for a superintendent. So, I went into the Board of Education conference room across the hall from my office to look at the pictures of all the superintendents before me. With the exception of the only woman who had a short Afro, they were all men in varying stages of baldness! Apparently, my hair needed to be much shorter to be appropriate, maybe even shaved off completely.

Once you understand the impact of rituals on creating a school culture, you can begin to move a school from harmful to healthy. The notion of creating rituals in your school community must be done with thoughtfulness by unpacking and uncovering those elements that comprise a school's culture and are sometimes not clear to the naked eye.

Meaningful and Transformational Routines

Routines establish structure. People depend on the routine to happen at a given month, day, or time and in a consistent manner. In *Corporate Cultures* by Deal and Kennedy (2000), "…while work rituals do not produce direct results, they are just as valuable because they provide a sense of security and common identity…"

This sense of security is crucial in developing the organizational narrative and establishing a leadership vision. Routines should be consistent and meaningful. Nothing is worse than "going through the motions" of a routine that has no collective meaning. Think about the routines educational organizations typically implement: daily pledge; signing in/out when arriving/leaving; assigning a specific parking spot; mandatory attendance at daily stand-up or zoom meetings; announcements over the public address system; bells for class change; holiday themed instruction or events; Homecoming; open houses; parent/teacher conferences; and the like.

Many years ago, I was fortunate to spend some time with Dr. Gary Phillips, founder and President of National School Improvement Project, Inc. His rule was, "Always leave people and places better than you found them." You can certainly replicate or continue with current routines, but imagine how powerful these routines could be if you made them about the way things *ought* to be. Phillips additionally stated that, "no schools can be changed without changing the rituals." Routines that are transformational and meaningful move the organization to a new level of potential. Think about developing routines that have a transformational quality.

When we opened a brand-new school—The Center for Language, Culture, and Communication Arts—we thought about what kind of opening ceremony would symbolize who we were as a school community. Traditionally, there is the ribbon-cutting event that lets everyone know the school is officially opened. But, since we were a school promoting cultural and racial diversity, we decided to do a ribbon-tying event. We had multiple ribbons taped to one wall of the gymnasium/cafeteria and invited representative members of our community to take one of the ribbons in their hands, meet the principal in the middle where all the ribbons would be tied together with a bow. This symbolized the uniting of our community and the launch of a new school identity.

One of the best ways to establish routines/rituals is to ask for suggestions and engage staff in their development. Ask them how they would like to start and end their day, what staff meetings should be about, what kind of identity they would like to project about their school/district, how they would like to make decisions, or how they are celebrated. Ask parents how they would like their children's day to begin, the best way for drop off and pick up from school, what conferences should look like and at what time of the day, field trips they might like to attend, or the agenda for parent meetings and open houses. Instead of rules, they become We Agree Covenants.

Whatever routines you establish, make them consistent and of high quality—a groove instead of a rut. Such as:

- a morning inspirational message
- a congratulatory remark to someone
- a weekly note in everyone's mailbox
- a positive Monday morning memo (more on this later)
- greet students and staff each morning in person
- begin staff meetings with positive statements from each person

- posting a question of the day outside the office area and in the hallways for students as they move through the school
- compliment instead of criticize

In both my positions at the Michigan Department of Education and as superintendent of an urban school district, I had a routine that I believe was transformational. It was called The Monday Morning Memo or M3:

Every Sunday evening, for years, I would sit at my computer and write a memo to all the staff. As superintendent, it went to all mailboxes and was posted on our district website. In general, it was an opportunity for me to recap the previous week and share what was on the horizon. It also served as a celebratory way of highlighting those staff, students, and/or community members or organizations that had done something special for the district. At times, it was simply a way for the community to know me better. During a few "dry" news times, I added a favorite recipe or two, opining on current topics, and sharing a few personal details about my life. Once, while in China, after having tumbled down The Great Wall, I included a picture of me and my broken ankle! The M3 didn't need to be all business; the personal side of leadership was also important to include. I think I must have apologized several times for calling snow days—no one is ever happy about that decision! No matter the weather or the location, I sent out that "Good Morning" to my community. Over the years, I think I must have written over 600 Monday Morning Memos. It was a ritual and an artifact that greeted people each Monday morning as they began their workweek. It was as much a ritual for me to write it as it was for the reader to expect it.

All of these routine rituals can make a big difference in developing a school or district identity.

Events as Rituals—
Transformational or
Traditional

We are organized by monthly holiday events, especially in schools. There's the Halloween Parade, the Thanksgiving breakfast, the Winter Carnival, homage to Dr. Martin Luther King, Jr., Valentine's Day, St. Patrick's Day, Spring Break, Memorial Day, and a final end-of-school-year celebration. These are all predictable and expected. However, there are ways to celebrate these events that are more transformational than traditional (see following table). From a cultural mindfulness standpoint, the majority of these traditional holidays have been generated by the dominant culture, with few representations of the rich heritage that nondominant people have contributed to our nation's cultural wealth. Inviting community members who are part of diverse racial and ethnic groups to participate in designing, developing, and implementing transformational events is important for leaders. Keep in mind that whenever you decide to change a traditional event or ritual, some people may not be in agreement.

Traditional	Transformational	Month
General Announcements	Character trait of the week. Read on PA. Share quotations or have students write and share their writings.	All Year
Start of School Year Assembly	Tie a Ribbon Pole to indicate partnerships.	September
	Draw or write about how you can be the best that you can be this year.	
Halloween Parade	Creative Art Gallery Walk that focuses on Latinx culture.	October
	Posters of local historical figures and events.	
Thanksgiving Breakfast with Pilgrims	End of season harvest with popcorn and thank-you notes to special people.	November
	Honor contributions of Native Americans.	
Christmas Program	Winter Wonderland songs and art.	December
	Create and distribute an Anthology of stories written by parents about holiday traditions.	
Martin Luther King, Jr. Day	Use both January and February for highlighting Black History.	January
Valentine's Day Party	Fill a bucket with heartfelt notes.	February
	Chinese/Lunar New Year Celebration.	
St. Patrick's Day with Leprechauns	Highlight the contributions of immigrants to the U.S.	March
Reading Month	Focus on authors/books about diverse cultures.	
Spring Break	Honoring Flora and Fauna.	April
	Celebrate Arbor Day by planting a tree.	
Earth Day	Create classroom murals or collages about how to take care of the earth.	

Mother's Day	Cards to mom or other women who have impacted students.	May
	Service Learning Project to support mothers.	
	Use the month for presentations by women.	
Memorial Day	Thank a veteran by writing letters or inviting them to speak to students.	
End of School Year	Honor all students and staff with a celebration.	June
	Assembly to give each staff member a flower and thank-you notes from students.	

High Schools continue to select a Homecoming Court, usually during football and basketball seasons—once in the fall and once in the late winter. With few exceptions, it is a popularity contest. However, there are high schools that are thinking very differently about these annual rituals. For example, Eastern High School in Lansing, Michigan, decided to have the student body elect a cadre of Eastern Quaker (mascot) Ambassadors—those students who embodied the principles, values, and beliefs of the school community. Kudos to them for breaking the mold and for making this ritual transformational.

Ritual events should be both predictable and unpredictable. There should be an expectation that a yearly culminating or benchmarking event will occur at the end of the school year, but it's also a good idea to add a couple of unpredictable events that set a new course for the school community's narrative. Unpredictable events can be a one-off kind that might not last much beyond the event. Make sure you understand which kind you are implementing. For example:

A small group of leaders from the business community decided to put their resources together and launch a Thanksgiving event during which food was given to those in need. They contacted the school district to discuss the idea and to think about how to determine those most in need. On the weekend before Thanksgiving, hundreds of volunteers came together in a high school parking lot for a drive-up distribution of food and clothing. It was a new ritual event that was greatly appreciated. It uplifted the community and left its mark for several years. Its continuance is dependent upon the generosity of community leaders.

Other predictable events include field trips. The Senior Trip was around when I was in high school 50 years ago! They still exist today although a school bus to Washington, D.C., has been supplanted by air travel to Punta Cana! There's an expectation that all seniors will celebrate their last year in high school with a big trip to somewhere. Even elementary school children expect a trip to an amusement park for having endured their school year. These are ritual events that aren't generally in the context of the school community's mission.

The field trip event should be in context and coherent with the stated mission. It's OK to have fun, to be sure, but wouldn't it be better to provide an experience that is innovative, instructional, and considers the prohibitive aspects of cost.

Suggestions for field trips:

Instead of	Think About
Amusement Park	Day camp learning about flora and fauna.
Water Park	Historical/Naval Museum with historical character writing in journals.
Video Game Center	Hire an artist to develop a school mural.
Beach Picnic	Hire a yoga or dance instructor to teach lifelong healthy movement.
Real Field Trip	Create a virtual field trip using cell phones to create individual student trips and post on approved social media platform.
Senior Trip	Community Service Learning Project. Week-long internship in each student's desired career.

Event rituals don't need to be big productions. They can be small, meaningful events for individuals or for smaller cohorts. Perhaps a grade level or math department schedules an event that is specifically related to a curricular study. Or, a community member wants to recognize and celebrate a student or staff member with flowers. These are small rituals that could be unpredictable, one-time events; or, they can be ones that are done on a regular basis. The point is that there are big, all-consuming rituals (like graduation ceremonies) and there are smaller, more targeted ritual events (perfect attendance student/classroom for a given month) and both contribute to the school community narrative.

Activities as Rituals

Throughout the school year, there are a myriad of activities that display and support the school's mission and culture. You might want to discuss the kinds of activities you will sponsor: academic and focused on student engagement or community-based that target a wider constituency.

Student/Academic Focus	Community-Based
Attendance recognition	Open House
Citizen of the month	Family Night
Honor Roll	School Carnival
Student Musical Performance	Diversity Fair
After school clubs, organizations	Community organization meeting

Remember that people are expecting these activities to be consistent and meaningful so once you start with a perfect attendance recognition, you need to decide how often you want to make the award. If it's yearly, it becomes more of a celebration; activities that are benchmarked throughout the school year are slightly less ceremonious, and usually predictable.

PODs Projects of Discovery Activities

Earlier, I shared information about a project that we developed at an elementary school based on Howard Gardner's research on multiple intelligences, called PODs or Projects of Discovery that replaced the dreaded lunchtime where one group of students eats while the other group is outside (usually playing in unstructured chaos), switching places midway through the lunch period. The old model of a 40-minute lunch period—20 minutes eating and 20 minutes outside—wasn't maximizing student engagement every day. Yes, teachers by contract, had a duty-free lunch; but students didn't! Naturally, the decision to make a change in a traditional routine had to be made collectively with the staff. They had to agree to this new way of doing things. There had to be advantages for both students and staff.

We created an alternative structure to the lunch period:

- There were four Lunch Modules, starting at 11 a.m., finishing at 1 p.m.
- Students in each module would eat for 15 minutes and then transition to a POD.
- There were five to seven PODs for each Lunch Module, ranging from 10–20 students in each POD.
- One POD would be outside with higher numbers of students in the lower grades, gradually decreasing in upper grades. Other PODs included a variety of indoor experiences.
- After three weeks, students would switch to a different set of PODs. At the end of the three-week period, they would provide a performance in an assembly or a gallery walk.
- Teachers rotated supervision of all PODs during the lunch period with extra pay.
- Volunteers and school staff instructed PODs.

There were several advantages to this activity:

- Students were exposed to unique learning outside of the regular curriculum
- A structured lunch period provided a predictable routine
- Fewer negative incidents took up valuable instructional time
- Reduced need for part-time lunch aides (these folks are very difficult to find!)
- Increased involvement by parents/community members
- Teachers received an extra 10 minutes of duty-free time

It was a lot to organize, but the benefits far outweighed the trouble. Try it! Maybe on a smaller scale, but I think you'll find it is worth the effort, especially if you partner with organizations in the community. You can find a template for PODs in the Activity Section at the end of this chapter.

Active Investment as Ritual

In Chapter One we looked at the importance of leaders building professional equity by being visible in the community. A powerful ritual can be
in the form of investing in, praising and rewarding your staff, students, and
community generously. They need to know from you, the leader, that you
believe they are of value—worth your time, worth your energy, worth
your investment in them. You need to attend sporting events, potlucks,
town halls, and fundraisers. The time you spend in the community within
which you are a leader tells the members of that community that they are
important to you. I've known school and district leaders who:

- Don't live in or near the community
- Rarely attend student athletic or performance events
- Don't contribute to fundraising efforts by community groups
- Can't seem to make a meatloaf for a potluck

People take notice of the amount of time and level of engagement you're
willing to contribute. It's all part of building your professional equity in the
community and demonstrating your sincere commitment to the community's overall well-being.

Putting notes in teachers' mailboxes is an important (and easy) way to
thank them and let them know they're valued. During negotiations, I would
give each staff member a 100 Grand chocolate bar with a little note: "Sorry
this isn't real, even though you're worth it!" Authentic recognition such as
compliments and thank-you notes are essential artifacts for making visible
the way things ought to be.

As superintendent, my executive team met every Thursday morning
for several hours to review the week and discuss what was on the
horizon. The meeting generally started at 9 a.m. and could last
until after lunchtime. I had a habit of baking goodies for the group
on Wednesday night or early Thursday morning to stave off hunger
during the meeting. Sometimes it was a new cake recipe, fruit with
yogurt, or cookies. One of my special treats was corn bread. To this
day, they remember the effort and the corn bread.

Artifacts

rtifacts as a form of rituals make visible the surface of a school's culture and can be easily seen by an outsider in a variety of ways. Those on the inside may just take them for granted and if they represent some historical narrative, may not be understood by those new to the "inside." Physical artifacts such as the decorations, space allocation, the way people dress, awards, trophies, handbooks, posters, mascots, logos, and symbols all tell a story about the organization's cultural values through a visual rendition of ritual.

Even architecture can tell a story about the instructional vision and culture of the organization. There's a wonderful book called *The Third Teacher* by O'Donnell, Wicklund, Pigozzi, and Peterson (OWP/P Architects) and Bruce Mau, highlighting that there is so much you can tell about the vision, values, and culture of a school based on the architecture of the building:

- Are there open collaborative spaces?
- Are hallways also used for instruction/tutorial?
- Are there dedicated spaces for displaying student work?
- Are there bright colors and natural lighting?
- Is the entrance open and inviting?
- Are environmental protections evident?

As superintendent, I used this book with our board of education and our architects when redesigning the many schools involved in a large district-wide bond project and provided it to school-level administrators as part of a book study initiative.

Physical artifacts tell the outsider who the insiders are, their identity and the ways in which they want their identity projected in a three-dimensional way.

At one point in my career, I had regionally located consultants working in schools and with school districts. Frequently, I would visit the staff and have them show me the "good" schools and the "struggling" schools—mostly because I was interested in knowing how they perceived good and struggling. One of the consultants brought me to a small high school she thought was doing very well. In the lobby there was an enormous glass case that held dozens of trophies. In the gymnasium, there was another enormous case with more trophies—for every sport and for all the years the school had been in existence. Throughout the halls there were other glass cases that were relatively empty, with minimal display of student work. We also visited a few classrooms. The biology room had a single microscope. I asked the consultant to share with me what she thought was important to this school's leadership. She said, "student learning." I asked her if she thought the physical artifacts expressed that assumption, noting the hundreds of trophies (which are costly) and the single microscope in the biology lab. She became defensive and said that the school didn't have the resources to equip every classroom. Eventually she admitted that sports were very important to that community because they brought people together. I replied that, "yes" it was clear that athletics were important.

You can tell a lot about a school by simply walking around. Dr. Phil Cusick would suggest just walking around, looking, and watching. Where are things located? Who is located where? What are the decorations? Do you see student work displayed? What seems to be important to this community? To this day, I can't walk into a school without first making observations about the physical artifacts illustrating the school's identity.

Language as Artifact

Language usage, or lexicon, is another way a school's culture is manifested through slogans, sayings, special expressions, and even the way people speak. Is the language free of racial and gender bias? Do people feel free to use their native language if it isn't English?

I worked in a junior high with a colleague who also spoke Spanish. Whenever we met, we naturally spoke to each other in the language that was most comfortable. Some people would hear us, even if we were quietly talking, and say, "stop talking about me." Why they thought we were spending any time talking about them was beyond me. It was code for saying, speak English only.

Are there unique codes or words that only the people inside the school's culture would know or use? Now retired Ricardo Briones was a popular principal of an elementary school who had his own school saying:

Be nice and work hard.

Simple and understood by all.

The principal of a large high school also had a saying that she used on a daily basis:

Make it a great day or not, the choice is yours!

Everyone knew it. It was sort of a rallying cry at the end of each meeting, at the end of pep rallies, at the end of a graduation speech. In fact, I couldn't remember the exact wording for this book, so I contacted a teacher who had been in that school a few years ago and she remembered it! That's an example of a lasting ritual.

Mine was:

Vision without implementation is hallucination.

Stories as Artifacts

Stories about your school and community are important for keeping the narrative alive. Not only do stories recall history, they <u>make</u> history as they are passed on (transmitted) to new members. In these stories, there are sometimes heroes and heroines who are highlighted. They can be progressive stories, meaning that each year they have additional narrative or they can be start-up stories. Either way, oral tradition is something that has been a part of cultural rituals for hundreds of years. Can you think of oral traditions in your own family or workplace?

While oral traditions in the form of stories serve an important purpose in the process of enculturation, these stories can also be written down and made into anthologies, thus becoming artifacts for the whole school population. An activity that I used with both parents and staff was to choose a writing theme and have them contribute their thoughts—on paper or in a recording. At the time, we put them all in a booklet, but now you can do an anthology video!

One of the wonderful stories that became part of an anthology on *Family Traditions* sponsored by the Parent Advisory Council of the school in which I was the principal came from a much-loved leader in the community and mentor of mine who has since passed away:

Tracing one's roots is becoming the thing to do, to give an individual a connection with the past and their heritage.

Immediately before the Civil War, people were moving across the country, and so were our ancestors. These old settlers moved from other states and Canada to Mecosta, Montcalm, and Isabella counties of Michigan. They came in covered wagons drawn by oxen. This was known as the end of the slave line.

Each year on the third Saturday in August, the descendants and friends of families who settled in the three-county area come together in memory of the pioneers who settled there. They acknowledge the oldest members, see the newest offspring, share family records, and renew acquaintances. This "Old Settlers Reunion" is held at School Section Lake Park area which was originally owned by John Berry, Senior. The names of the family members appear on a monument in the park.

I am privileged to have the knowledge of the struggles and hardships of my ancestors; they provide me with the incentive to help make their dreams come true.

Richard D. Letts, Retired Director of Human Relations, City of Lansing

This next story is one to which many of us can relate. From a wonderful teacher, Amy Yenter-Chavez, came this memorable life ritual:

Oh how I remember the delicious aroma of bacon and the crackling of eggs frying and the melodic tenor voice of my father singing a Polish song. In my family, for as long as I can remember, it was my father who was in charge of Sunday morning breakfast. Whether it was his way of helping my mother by giving her some free time, or his desire to get behind a pan and spatula, I have no idea. But, I somehow believe that he really enjoyed this change of role because he always had a little smile on his face and sang or hummed a happy tune while at work. The eggs he made were just perfect: done over easy, not too hard, not too soft, a touch of salt and a generous sprinkling of pepper. No one makes eggs like my father! The eggs were always accompanied by lightly toasted bread that one of the kids was in charge of. At times, he included crisp bacon or juicy pork sausages or even salty ham. But those eggs were the main attraction. Even today, I can't find any eggs that can compare to the memory of my father's eggs.

His little Polish song still sticks in our minds like it was only yesterday. It was a song about a little dog walking down the road. The Polish words called our attention into fascination. Our father was speaking a different language and had spoken both Polish and Norwegian as a child! At one of our last family gatherings, my sister and I started to sing his song and my father couldn't believe his ears! We recalled almost all of the words. He laughed at our poorly spoken Polish but praised us for our efforts. He never realized that we would internalize his Sunday morning demeanor with great importance.

Now on Sunday, the bacon has turned into the spicy smell of chorizo sizzling in the pan, later to be mixed with eggs. Mmmmm, huevos con chorizo! The spatula and pan are now manned by my dear husband who also enjoys the talk and the idea of giving me some time off. The songs heard by our children are not in Polish, but now in Spanish. I hope that someday our children will look back on Sunday morning and remember their father with the same fond memories that I recall of my father in the kitchen on Sunday mornings because, after all, I still miss those wonderful eggs!

There are so many other venues for your community stories with the multiple platforms on social media. As superintendent, I engaged our team in producing a "welcome back to school" video each year as part of our cultural narrative. It was fun to produce and staff seemed to enjoy the yearly ritual for opening the school year.

Vision is more than a poster. In fact, a poster is definitely not enough for your school community to faithfully live its vision. It needs to be tangible, concrete, in song, in sayings, in images, in video, three-dimensional, and collaboratively implemented. Even the cleanliness and organization of a school tells so much about what is valued by the members of that community and of the leader.

A common ritual artifact of a school's culture is the Mission Statement. It is used to announce to the school community the core values of the school or district's mission—always about nurturing and supporting students.

As I wandered the halls of a public elementary school one day, I noticed that above the door to the gymnasium/cafeteria was a poster with the school's mission statement in big letters: We believe that all students can learn in a safe and nurturing environment that is student-centered, participatory, and inclusive of the diversity of our community. As I walked into the gymnasium, I noticed the students were eating lunch. No one was talking. The principal, dressed in full monk's trappings (rope belt included, like a Franciscan Friar) was walking around supervising and telling students to be quiet, as if they were in a cloistered order. This weekly event was actually called Monk's Lunch. I thought about the incongruity between the mission statement and what I observed, lunch being one of the only times students could freely converse with their friends, not to mention the religious presumption.

Rituals form the under-the-surface foundation of a school's culture and provide every leader the opportunity to make her/his vision come to life on a daily basis. Rituals give life to a school or district's cultural narrative through meaningful routines, events, activities, and artifacts in many ways. Every culture evolves and is dynamic; leaders have an opportunity to help shape the culture in which s/he works by being intentional about the rituals created, the routines established, the events and activities launched, and the artifacts produced and/or displayed.

Quotes that Inspire Leaders

Choose a quote that represents a quality that you feel is important in a leader or that reflects your personal philosophy of leadership, write about it, and/or share it with a colleague.

Write the quote and display it in a prominent place that will remind you of this perspective. Use as a tagline in your email signature.

Rituals:

- Leadership is the capacity to translate vision into reality. *Warren G. Bennis*

- We are what we repeatedly do. Excellence then is not an act, but a habit. *Will Durant*

- A leader takes people where they want to go. A great leader takes people where they don't necessarily want to go, but ought to be. *Rosalynn Carter*

- These were her rituals, the routines that made her feel alive and connected. Without them, where would she be? Lost. *Ben Sherwood*

- How you start your day is how you live your day. How you live your day is how you live your life. *Louise Hay*

- What you do every day matters more than what you do once in a while. *Gretchen Rubin*

- I like having a routine, because everything else…is so unpredictable. *Jordana Brewster*

- With him, life was routine; without him, life was unbearable. *Harper Lee*

- Serious writers write, inspired or not. Over time they discover that routine is a better friend than inspiration. *Ralph Keyes*

- Repetition is the mother of learning, the father of action, which makes it the architect of accomplishment. *Zig Ziglar*

- Practice is the best of all instructors. *Publilius Syrus*

- The difference between ordinary and extraordinary is practice. *Vladimir Horowitz*

- Success doesn't just come and find you. You have to go out and get it. *Anonymous*

- The more you praise and celebrate your life, the more there is in life to celebrate. *Oprah Winfrey*

Rituals

ACTIVITIES

KEY TO ACTIVITIES AND JOURNAL

VIGNETTE

LEADER ONLY

STAFF/TEAM

Rituals Activity 1: Environmental Scan Observations

Here are a few of the *cultural influences* that you would observe and take note of when analyzing the school or district environment. *Use the Comments section to record your insights. See Activity 2 for help on definitions.*

Use of Space—*this requires you to observe by walking about to record your findings.*

Cultural Influences	Comments
Location of	
• *Classrooms*	
• *Office*	
• *Media Center*	
• *Cafeteria*	
• *Staff Lounge*	
• *Parent/Volunteer Room*	
• *Public Gathering Spaces*	
Level of Cleanliness	
Ease of Access for Public	
Parking Lot (designated spaces)	
Other influences noticed	

Use of Resources—*this requires you to observe by walking about to record your findings.*

Cultural Influences	Comments
Shared Items	
• *Computers*	
• *Printers*	
• *Paper, construction/copy/lined*	
• *Pencils, crayons, markers*	
• *Kitchen appliances*	
• *Furniture*	
• *Telephones*	
Physical Education Equipment	
Art/Music Supplies	
Budget Allocation Line Items	
Other influences noticed	

Communication Norms—*this requires you to be a limited participant observer or active listener to record your findings.*

Cultural Influences	Comments
Shared Language	
Greetings Used or Posted	
Personal vs. Professional Conversations *(frequency)*	
Language used by and about	
• *Supervisors/Leadership*	
• *Students*	
• *Colleagues*	
• *Community*	
Other influences noticed	

Identity and Image—*this requires you to observe by walking about to record your findings.*

Cultural Influences	Comments
Signage	
Images of Identity	
Visible Artifacts	
Display of Student Work	
Posting of Rules/Norms	
Representations of Diversity	
Dress of Staff	
Dress of Students	
Dress of Families	
Other influences noticed	

©*Environmental Scan. Yvonne Caamal Canul. 8.2020*

Rituals Activity 2:
Elements of School Culture

Think about the rituals that are meaningful to the staff in your school community.

Element	Description of Current Practice	Modify (Y/N)	Modification
Mission (why)			
Images/Identity			
Values/Beliefs			
Special Rituals			
Daily Routines			
Ceremonies			
Norms			
Behavioral Expectations			
Story of the School/District			
Hero/Heroine			
Special Language			
Climate			

©*Elements of School Culture. Yvonne Caamal Canul. 8.2020*

Definitions:

- **Mission:** Why your school/district exists and for whom and what you intend to do for them.
- **Images/Identity:** The symbols, pictures you use to let people know who you are.
- **Values/Beliefs:** Statements that crystalize all that is really important to them.
- **Special Rituals:** Activities that you perform that are unique to your school community.
- **Daily Routines:** Activities that you perform habitually.
- **Ceremonies:** Celebratory events that are unique to your school community.
- **Norms:** Unwritten rules that provide standards of process and protocols.
- **Behavioral Expectations:** Written or unwritten ways in which people are expected to behave.
- **Story of the School/District:** Historical narrative that is unique to your school community.
- **Hero or Heroine:** Someone who represents the identity of your school community in a positive way.
- **Special Language:** Words that are unique to your school community, nicknames, jargon, and/or abbreviations. Acknowledge importance of other languages.
- **Climate:** The general mood of the school community.

Elements of School Culture—Rituals Journal

Choose three elements that I identified as wanting to modify and why.

1.

2.

3.

What steps will I take to begin?

How will I engage staff/my team?

After reviewing the list of routines, are there any that I want to add?

Rituals Activity 3: All for One

Look at the following statements and decide the extent to which this represents your school community.

Statement	Always	Usually	Rarely	Never
There are clear and common values, beliefs, protocols, or routines.				
There is agreement on what's important.				
Different departments/units in the school/district have different beliefs, protocols, routines, and processes.				
Leadership seeks common understanding.				
Routines are meaningful, organized, consistent, and coherent.				
The school/district has an inward focus, refusing to be distracted by external factors.				
Focus is long term with common strategies, routines, or protocols.				
Morale is high.				
Staff publicly display their frustration.				
Staff use social media to air their concerns.				
Parents and community members are recognized for their contributions to the school community.				
Staff are recognized for their unique contributions to the school community.				

©All for One. Yvonne Caamal Canul. 8.2020

Suggested Activity

- Administer this survey with your staff and use for discussion to take the "temperature" of your school/district culture.
- Share your responses to this survey to compare points of view.
- Convene a committee to develop a plan to improve shared understanding in your school community.
- Use their answers to the survey for a Collective Growth Plan.

Rituals Activity 3:
Survey of All for One

Indicate the extent to which you believe these statements are reflective of your school community.

Statement	Always	Usually	Rarely	Never
There are clear and common values, beliefs, protocols, or routines.				
There is agreement on what's important.				
Different departments/units in the school/district have different beliefs, protocols, routines, and processes.				
Leadership seeks common understanding.				
Routines are meaningful, organized, consistent, and coherent.				
The school/district has an inward focus, refusing to be distracted by external factors.				
Focus is long term with common strategies, routines, or protocols.				
Morale is high.				
Staff publicly display their frustration.				
Staff use social media to air their concerns.				
Parents and community members are recognized for their contributions to the school community.				
Staff are recognized for their unique contributions to the school community.				

©All for One. Yvonne Caamal Canul. 8.2020

All for One—Relationships Journal

Ask your staff/team to reflect on the following:

Three observations to which staff answered "rarely" or "never."

    1.

    2.

    3.

Three observations to which staff answered "always" or "usually."

    1.

    2.

    3.

What patterns or trends emerged?

From the discussion with our designated committee about how to improve our school culture, we will add these three actions to our Collective Growth Plan.

    1.

    2.

    3.

Rituals Activity 4:
Survey of School Norms

From this list of (implicit) school norms, decide the extent to which each is relevant to your school community.

School Norm STAFF....	Always	Usually	Rarely	Never	Not observed
Treat all people with respect.					
Feel a sense of responsibility for student learning.					
Are willing to take on extra responsibilities.					
Agree with the principal.					
Encourage those who suggest new ideas.					
Don't make waves.					
Are conscious of costs and the use of resources.					
Speak with pride about the school.					
Believe they are rewarded/recognized based on politics.					
Are helpful and supportive of all others.					
View parents as an important asset.					
Share useful information and new ideas.					
Solve problems together.					
Criticize those who try different things.					
Place needs of students as first priority.					
Complain about little things all the time.					
Find ways to expand their own learning.					
Put personal needs over school needs.					
Are trustful, authentic, honest.					

© School Norms. Yvonne Caamal Canul. 8.2020

Suggested Activity

- Share your responses to this survey with your staff/team and use for discussion about the extent to which your collective school norms are evident in your school environment.
- Give this survey to your staff/team for discussion about how to improve school culture.
- Use their answers to the survey for a Collective Growth Plan.

Rituals Activity 4:
Survey of School Norms

Indicate the extent to which these norms are evident in our school community.

School Norm STAFF….	Always	Usually	Rarely	Never	Not observed
Treat all people with respect.					
Feel a sense of responsibility for student learning.					
Are willing to take on extra responsibilities.					
Agree with the principal.					
Encourage those who suggest new ideas.					
Don't make waves.					
Are conscious of costs and the use of resources.					
Speak with pride about the school.					
Believe they are rewarded/recognized based on politics.					
Are helpful and supportive of all others.					
View parents as an important asset.					
Share useful information and new ideas.					
Solve problems together.					
Criticize those who try different things.					
Place needs of students above personal.					
Complain about little things all the time.					
Find ways to expand their own learning.					
Put personal needs over school needs.					
Are trustful, authentic, honest.					

© *School Norms. Yvonne Caamal Canul. 8.2020*

School Norms—Rituals Journal

Three observations to which staff answered "rarely," "never," or "not observed."

   1.

   2.

   3.

Three observations to which staff answered "always" or "usually."

   1.

   2.

   3.

What patterns or trends emerged?

From the staff/team discussion about how to improve school culture, we will add these three actions to our Collective Growth Plan.

   1.

   2.

   3.

Rituals Activity 5:
Basic Assumptions Inventory

Indicate the extent to which you believe these assumptions are evident in your school community.

Assumption	Always	Usually	Rarely	Never
Truth, no matter the cost, is an important aspect of our school culture.				
The time we spend in staff meetings is meaningful.				
Schedules for professional learning take into consideration the interests of the participants.				
Parent Teacher conferences are held at different times for parent convenience.				
Classroom assignments are made collaboratively with school leadership.				
Members of this school community are allowed to decorate their work areas.				
Everyone who works here knows each other.				
Individual space is respected.				
People speak at a volume level that is appropriate for indoor spaces.				
People here honor the "cone of silence."				
Everyone here believes that all students can achieve.				
We believe that all parents care about their child's education.				
Work and play ratios are appropriate.				
People here are recognized on merit.				
Individual interests are respected.				
Decisions are made collaboratively.				
Everyone's voice is valued.				
We are more collaborative than competitive.				
Everyone knows the dress code.				

© *Basic Assumptions. Yvonne Caamal Canul.8. 2020*

Suggested Activity

- Share this survey with your staff and use for discussion about the extent to which your basic assumptions are evident in your school environment.
- Give this survey to your team for discussion about how to improve school culture. Use their answers for the Collective Growth Plan.
- Rituals Activity 5: Survey of Assumptions for Staff
- Indicate the extent to which you believe these assumptions are evident in our school community.

Rituals Activity 5:
Basic Assumptions Inventory

Indicate the extent to which you believe these assumptions are evident in your school community.

Assumption	Always	Usually	Rarely	Never
Truth, no matter the cost, is an important aspect of our school culture.				
The time we spend in staff meetings is meaningful.				
Schedules for professional learning take into consideration the interests of the participants.				
Parent Teacher conferences are held at different times for parent convenience.				
Classroom assignments are made collaboratively with school leadership.				
Members of this school community are allowed to decorate their work areas.				
Everyone who works here knows each other.				
Individual space is respected.				
People speak at a volume level that is appropriate for indoor spaces.				
People here honor the "cone of silence."				
Everyone here believes that all students can achieve.				
We believe that all parents care about their child's education.				
Work and play ratios are appropriate.				
People here are recognized on merit.				
Individual interests are respected.				
Decisions are made collaboratively.				
Everyone's voice is valued.				
We are more collaborative than competitive.				
Everyone knows the dress code.				

© Basic Assumptions. Yvonne Caamal Canul.8. 2020

Staff/Team Basic Assumptions—Rituals Journal

Three observations to which staff answered "rarely" or "never."

1.

2.

3.

Three observations to which staff answered "always" or "usually."

1.

2.

3.

What patterns or trends emerged?

From the staff /team discussion about how to improve school culture, we will add these three actions to our Collective Growth Plan.

1.

2.

3.

Rituals Activity 6: Meeting Norms

Think about the following examples of Ground Rules for meetings and check the ones you already use or plan to use in the future.

Ground Rule	Already Use	Plan to Use
Be Present		
No Drama		
Bring Problems with Potential Solutions		
Cone of Silence		
PEDs OFF		
Listen for Understanding		
Don't Interrupt		
Be Punctual		
Be Prepared		
Use Humor, Have Some Fun		
No Sidebars		
Be Additive Not Repetitive		
Be Respectful		
Bird Walking is Acceptable if Relevant		
Make Space for Discomfort		
Respect Air Time–No One Dominates		

©Meeting Norms. Yvonne Caamal Canul. 8.2020

How will ground rules be identified?

- ☐ Leader identifies rules that are indicative of the leader's style.

- ☐ Leader convenes the group, provides input on preferred rules, and asks for others the group might want.

- ☐ Leader asks the group to identify ground rules they want.

How and when will ground rules be used?

- ☐ At every meeting, including with the community?

- ☐ When a ground rule is broken, is there correction? How is it corrected and who decides?

- ☐ Does the group provide ground rules "orientation" to new members of the group?

Rituals Activity 6:
Meeting Norms

Consider these questions and suggestions for developing meeting norms:

Ground Rule	Already Use	Plan to Use
Be Present		
No Drama		
Bring Problems with Potential Solutions		
Cone of Silence		
PEDs OFF		
Listen for Understanding		
Don't Interrupt		
Be Punctual		
Be Prepared		
Use Humor, Have Some Fun		
No Sidebars		
Be Additive Not Repetitive		
Be Respectful		
Bird Walking is Acceptable if Relevant		
Make Space for Discomfort		
Respect Air Time–No One Dominates		

How will ground rules be identified?

☐ Leader identifies rules that are indicative of the leader's style.

☐ Leader convenes the group, provides input on preferred rules, and asks for others the group might want.

☐ Leader asks the group to identify ground rules they want.

How and when will ground rules be used?

☐ At every meeting, including with the community?

☐ When a ground rule is broken, is there correction? How is it corrected and who decides?

☐ Does the group provide ground rules "orientation" to new members of the group?

Staff/Team Meeting Norms—Rituals Journal

Three meeting norms we already use.

1.

2.

3.

Three meeting norms we plan to use in the future.

1.

2.

3.

Three meeting norms we can't live without.

1.

2.

3.

How and when will we use the norms?

What is the correction if the norm is broken?

Rituals Activity 7: Survey Cultural Competencies— Representation

Indicate the extent to which you believe these statements are evident in the school.

Consider the following	Always	Usually	Rarely	Never
Staff can accurately name and identify the racial, ethnic, and/or linguistic groups represented in the community.				
Committees for organizational events and programs reflect the diversity of the people in the school community.				
Mascots, emblems, team names, and awards are free from racial, ethnic, linguistic, spiritual, and gender bias.				
Symbols used within the school community are reflective of cultural diversity.				
Important events are reflective of racial, ethnic, linguistic, spiritual, physical, and gender diversity.				
Foods served in the school reflect community diversity.				
Artifacts, publications, presentations, decorations, instructional themes reflect racial, ethnic, linguistic, spiritual, physical, and gender diversity.				
Learning content integrates racial, ethnic, linguistic, spiritual, physical, and gender perspectives.				
Guest speakers/presenters reflect racial, ethnic, linguistic, spiritual, physical, and gender diversity.				

The professional library includes print materials that reflect racial, ethnic, linguistic, physical, and gender diversity.				
Media used by the organization reflects racial, ethnic, linguistic, physical, and gender diversity.				
Clubs include members from all racially, ethnically, linguistically, physically, and gender diverse groups.				
Parent/community advisory boards and committees represent the diversity of the school community.				

©*Survey of Cultural Perspectives. Yvonne Caamal Canul. 2008*

Suggested Activity

- Share this survey with your staff and use for discussion about the extent to which your collective cultural competencies are evident in your school community.
- Give this survey to your team for discussion about how to improve cultural proficiency. Use their answers for the Collective Growth Plan.

Rituals Activity 7: Staff Survey Cultural Competencies—Representation

Indicate the extent to which you believe these statements are evident in the school.

Consider the following	Always	Usually	Rarely	Never
Staff can accurately name and identify the racial, ethnic, and/or linguistic groups represented in the community.				
Committees for organizational events and programs reflect the diversity of the people in the school community.				
Mascots, emblems, team names, and awards are free from racial, ethnic, linguistic, spiritual, and gender bias.				
Symbols used within the school community are equitably reflective of cultural diversity.				
Important events are reflective of racial, ethnic, linguistic, spiritual, physical, and gender diversity.				
Foods served in the school reflect community diversity.				
Artifacts, publications, presentations, decorations, instructional themes reflect racial, ethnic, linguistic, spiritual, physical, and gender diversity.				
Learning content integrates racial, ethnic, linguistic, spiritual, physical, and gender perspectives.				
Guest speakers/presenters reflect racial, ethnic, linguistic, spiritual, physical, and gender diversity.				

The professional library includes print materials that reflect racial, ethnic, linguistic, physical, and gender diversity.				
Media used by the organization reflects racial, ethnic, linguistic, physical, and gender diversity.				
Clubs include members from all racially, ethnically, linguistically, physically, and gender diverse groups.				
Parent/community advisory boards and committees represent the diversity of the school community.				

©*Survey of Cultural Perspectives. Yvonne Caamal Canul. 2008*

Suggested Activity

Use answers to the inventory for the Collective Growth Plan.

Staff/Team Cultural Competencies—
Representation
Rituals Journal

Three observations to which staff/team answered "rarely" or "never."

    1.

    2.

    3.

Three observations to which staff/team answered "always" or "usually."

    1.

    2.

    3.

What patterns or trends emerged?

From our staff/team discussion about cultural proficiency, we will add these three actions to our Collective Growth Plan.

    1.

    2.

    3.

Rituals Activity 8:
Contemplating a Vignette

 In this book, a vignette is an italicized paragraph with a story that brings reality to the concepts addressed. There are several vignettes in this chapter on Rituals. As you think about each vignette, choose one that sparked a thought or insight and consider the following questions:

The vignette I have selected is about:

The reason I chose this vignette is because:

An insight I gleaned from this vignette was:

Rituals Activity 9:
Lunchtime PODs—
Projects of Discovery

Below is an example of how PODs were organized in a school as an alternative to the traditional lunchtime.

Group	Lunch Module	Time	# Students	Activity
Kinder & 1st	Module 1 A	11:00 – 11:15	120	Eating/Transition
	Module 1 B	11:20 – 11:50	120	POD–5 inside: 75, 1 outside: 45
2nd & 3rd	Module 2 A	11:20 – 11:35	150	Eating/Transition
	Module 2 B	11:40 – 12:10	150	POD–6 inside: 90; 1 outside: 60
4th & 5th	Module 3 A	11:40 – 11:55	125	Eating/Transition
	Module 3 B	12:00 – 12:30	125	POD–6 inside: 90; 1 outside: 35
6th	Module 4 A	12:00 – 12:15	50	Eating/Transition
	Module 4 B	12:20 – 12:50	50	POD–4 inside: 40; 1 outside: 10

- Module 1: Kinder – 3 classrooms of 20 = 60; 1st grade – 3 classrooms of 20= 60
- Module 2: 2nd grade – 3 classrooms of 25 = 75; 3rd grade – 3 classrooms of 25 = 75
- Module 3: 4th grade – 3 classrooms of 25 = 75; 5th grade – 2 classrooms of 25 = 50
- Module 4: 6th grade - 2 classrooms of 25 = 50

Inside PODs: Dance, Creative Writing, Spanish/French language class, internet time, American Sign Language, Arts and Crafts, Singing, Instrumental Music, nutrition class.

Outside PODs: Nature Walk, Soccer, Kickball, and other organized outside games.

Supervised by one teacher for each three-week POD series. Extra hours paid, lunch with Module 1 Eating OR Module 4 POD. Teachers rotated POD supervision. When teachers supervise the PODs, some of the time counted as "instructional." Each entire Module was 50 minutes.

POD Instructors are volunteers with honorariums and/or school staff who would eat after all Modules finished.

©Yvonne Caamal Canul. 8.2020

PODs—
Projects of Discovery
Template

Below is an example of a template that you can use to organize an alternative to the traditional lunchtime.

My Project of Discovery (PODs) Plan

Group	Lunch Module	Time	# Students	Activity
A	Module 1 A			Eating/Transition
	Module 1 B			POD–Inside: Outside:
B	Module 2 A			Eating/Transition
	Module 2 B			POD–Inside: Outside:
C	Module 3 A			Eating/Transition
	Module 3 B			POD–Inside: Outside:
D	Module 4 A			Eating/Transition
	Module 4 B			POD–Inside: Outside:

- Module 1:

- Module 2:

- Module 3:

- Module 4:

What are options for Inside PODs?

What are options for Outside PODs?

How will I compensate teachers/assistants/volunteers?

What are the strengths of this plan?

What are the challenges of this plan?

Growth Plans

Growth Plans

LEADER GROWTH PLAN

COLLECTIVE GROWTH PLAN

Growth Plans are designed to capture the data generated by the Activities; both Leader Activities and Staff or Team Activities. The leader is the "scribe" who will input the information into all Growth Plans and use them to develop and implement a positive school culture.

Leader Growth Plan—
Using Observation Data to Improve

Using the observation data that you have from the four surveys, choose three statements from each area and develop a growth plan. *(Note: answers provided are **examples only**)*

	Identify three areas for growth in each category.	What does this look like? What will you do?	How and when will you integrate this into your leadership style?	How will you know when you have achieved your goals?
Leadership Growth Reflection Observations	My why is displayed in my workspace.	Think and reflect on my purpose. Write it out in a succinct statement, frame it and post where all can see.	First week of school–review periodically–walk the talk.	I will be able to express my why and base my decisions on my why.
Leadership Growth Relationships Observations	I am comfortable in situations that challenge my perspective.	I will reflect on points of view that are different than my own. I will presume positive intentions and make an effort to understand others' perspectives by conversing with the individual and not taking it personally.	I will share this goal with team after activity has been completed. Encourage staff to share their perspectives. Work to be open for feedback.	Team will feel comfortable sharing divergent opinions. I will be more accepting of others' perspectives. Our team effort will be stronger.
School Community Growth Rituals Observations	Staff are recognized for their unique contributions to the school community.	Staff will individually be recognized for specific contributions. Survey staff about what is important to them. Find ways to recognize for individual successes. Keep track of what works for each.	Administer survey at beginning of school year. Give frequent, specific feedback when it is evident throughout the year.	Individuals will feel valued and supported, motivated to try new ideas. This will transfer to students.

©*Growth Plan. Betty Underwood. 8.2020*

Leader Growth Plan— Using Observations to Improve

Using the observation data that you have from the four surveys, choose three statements from each area and develop a growth plan.

	Identify three areas for growth in each category.	What does this look like? What will you do?	How and when will you integrate this into your leadership style?	How will you know when you have achieved your goals?
Leadership Growth Reflection Observations				
Leadership Growth Relationships Observations				
School Community Growth Rituals Observations				

©Betty Underwood. 8.2020

Observations in Relationships—
Collective Growth Plan

Using the response data from the surveys, develop a Collective Growth Plan.

Growth Plan	Statements answered as "Never"	Statements answered as "Rarely"
Goals for Growth		
Strategies for Growth		
Activities Supporting Strategies		
Evidence of Goal Success		

©*Collective Growth Plan. Yvonne Caamal Canul. 10.20*

Elements of School Culture— Collective Growth Plan

Using the response data from the surveys, develop a Collective Growth Plan.

Growth Plan	Statements answered as "Never"	Statements answered as "Rarely"
Goals for Growth		
Strategies for Growth		
Activities Supporting Strategies		
Evidence of Goal Success		

©Collective Growth Plan. Yvonne Caamal Canul. 10.20

All for One—
Collective Growth Plan

Using the response data from the surveys, develop a Collective Growth Plan.

Growth Plan	Statements answered as "Never"	Statements answered as "Rarely"
Goals for Growth		
Strategies for Growth		
Activities Supporting Strategies		
Evidence of Goal Success		

©*Collective Growth Plan. Yvonne Caamal Canul. 10.20*

School Norms—
Collective Growth Plan

Using the response data from the surveys, develop a Collective Growth Plan.

Growth Plan	Statements answered as "Never"	Statements answered as "Rarely"
Goals for Growth		
Strategies for Growth		
Activities Supporting Strategies		
Evidence of Goal Success		

©*Collective Growth Plan. Yvonne Caamal Canul. 10.20*

Basic Assumptions—
Collective Growth Plan

Using the response data from the surveys, develop a Collective Growth Plan.

Growth Plan	Statements answered as "Never"	Statements answered as "Rarely"
Goals for Growth		
Strategies for Growth		
Activities Supporting Strategies		
Evidence of Goal Success		

©*Collective Growth Plan. Yvonne Caamal Canul. 10.20*

Cultural Competencies—
Collective Growth Plan

Using the response data from the surveys, develop a Collective Growth Plan.

Growth Plan	Statements answered as "Never"	Statements answered as "Rarely"
Goals for Growth		
Strategies for Growth		
Activities Supporting Strategies		
Evidence of Goal Success		

©*Collective Growth Plan. Yvonne Caamal Canul. 10.20*

Appendix

MORE THOUGHTS ON LEADERSHIP

The following is a speech I presented at the annual Lighting the Path Women's Leadership Luncheon sponsored by the Capital Area United Way in 2016. I was asked to share lessons learned during my career as a woman leader. Perhaps you will find some sage advice within.

~~~~~~~~~~~~~~~~~~~~~~~~~~~~~~~~~~~~~~~

Good Afternoon. Thank you so much for inviting me to join you today. I am really honored and am hopeful you will not regret this decision as I divulge bits and pieces of my path to this podium. For me, this luncheon is one of the highlights of the year. To be among women leaders who are committed to lighting the path for others, is just so inspiring.

Speaking of Pathways… Wow, what an evening we had last night! The mandate from our community in passing the Pathway Promise bond proposal by over 60 percent is a defining moment for our district. This is a vote for our students who richly deserve the best we have to offer. Thank you, thank you, thank you.

I'm old. Almost ready for full retirement according to Social Security. This is a long story but I'll try to break it up in three major categories:

- Who I am and how I arrived in Lansing
- Why I decided to be an educator
- What I believe about leadership, especially for women

I'll tell some stories along the way and share vignettes of what impacted my development and highlight a few of the lessons learned. So, let's get started.

Who I Am and How I Arrived in Lansing

My birth name is Yvonne Marie Goudreault. My father's family was French-Canadian and Algonquin Indian from northern Quebec. They arrived in New Hampshire around 1907. My mother's family was from the Dolomite Mountains in northern Italy. They arrived in Battle Creek around 1922. Both my parents were raised speaking their family's native language—French and Italian. We're polyglots. My mother, Giovanna, one of 6 children, went to the University of Michigan where she majored in Spanish. My father, Fernand, one of 13 children, went to Sacred Heart in Montreal to be a cleric. He left the order at the age of 28, and landed in Vicksburg, Michigan, where he met my mother. Both were teachers. Mom taught Spanish and Geography, Dad taught French and English.

They were married at St. Mary's Cathedral here in Lansing. My dad was then a counselor at Boys Training School, my mom a teacher at Eastern High School. I used to walk down Pennsylvania Avenue with MSU Basketball Coach Forrdy Anderson's son to Mrs. Fink's preschool when I was four.

- **Lesson Learned: Pick nice people to walk you to school.**

I spent my kindergarten year in the classroom's doll house because I could write my name and knew the letters of the alphabet. The teacher told me that I couldn't outshine the other kids so she stashed me away until everybody caught up. That took a while. The teacher probably had good reason. My mother used to tell this story about me when I was four that made her realize she was in for a long haul with her daughter.

Apparently, the two little boys next door came to her one day complaining about me bossing them around. She sat me down and said that I should stop telling Andy and Charlie what to do because it wasn't nice. According to her, I replied, "Well, if they had any ideas of their own, I wouldn't have to boss them around!"

- **Lesson Learned: Don't boss little boys around.**

My brother, Paul, was born when I was five. My father was being heavily recruited by the United States Foreign Service. He spoke French, the diplomatic language in the fifties, and he was Catholic, apparently an uncommon religion among bureaucrats. My dad was adventurous and loved new challenges. We were sent to Fortaleza, Brazil—three degrees north of the equator. This is where I spent influential formative years and where I learned Portuguese. Every day we ate black beans and rice sprinkled with manioc flour. We danced at Carnival—I still remember the songs we'd sing. I learned that the color of a person's skin does not define the content of their character. I also saw poverty and the effects of failed U.S. foreign policies.

This region, where 2 percent of the people had money and 98 percent were living in squalor, was in the middle of a growing communist movement and at one point my dad disappeared for a period of time. As the only U.S. diplomat in the region, he had been targeted by anti-American organizations. No rain had fallen for over two years and people were dying from the drought. My dad would greet the C130s flying in from the U.S. carrying subsidized cheese and powdered milk, but without water it's kind of hard to make milk from a powder and cheese isn't part of the diet in northeastern Brazil. We had bodyguards and chauffeurs; maids had to be carefully watched.

One night when I was about 7, my parents went out for an event and I was left "in charge" of the house. My mom used to say, "When I'm not here, you're the lady of the house." I took that responsibility pretty seriously. Well, on this night, the cook and the babysitter got into a fight over who was going to take care of my little brother that evening. The cook said she was a cook, not a babysitter. The babysitter said she was tired of taking care of my brother and needed a break. They started to fight. The babysitter grabbed a knife and threatened to kill the cook. So, I stepped in and fired the babysitter.

We needed a cook more than a babysitter. She left unceremoniously and without incident. When my parents returned, they asked me what happened to Ruth. I told them I had fired her.

- **Lesson Learned: Be decisive in the face of disaster.**

Years later my father was given honorary citizenship in the state of Ceará. He proudly hung that certificate all the days of his life. The next assignment was Guadalajara, México.

We returned to the U. S. for a brief time when I was in third grade where I learned quite assuredly that I would be living between two worlds the rest of my life. When I arrived in Brazil after kindergarten, the teacher asked us to draw a tree. I drew an apple tree. Got a zero. No apple trees in northeastern Brazil. When I came back to the U.S., my third grade teacher asked us to draw a tree. I got it, I thought. I drew a palm tree. Another zero. So apple tree or palm tree, wherever I am, they're in my heart.

- **Lesson Learned: There's more than one type of tree on this planet.**

The next assignment was Santiago, Chile. Metropolitan city of 3 million people nestled in a valley in the Andes Mountains. I loved Chile. It is truly one of the most beautiful countries in the world. Given that the seasons are the opposite there, I arrived in the middle of the school year but seemed to fit right in with other kids whose parents worked for the Embassies and foreign trade programs. The Beatles were exploding on the music scene and I was a big fan, as were all my girlfriends. Here I learned Spanish and decided that my life would evolve as a Chilean. I had my university selected, my boyfriend was chosen, I knew where I wanted to live. It was all settled. Then, the Marxist was elected president and we packed up rather quickly, boarded a boat with our belongings and sailed home for the last time. To Olivet, Michigan, where my father took a position as a professor.

- **Lesson Learned: Enjoy the journey because plans can change unexpectedly.**

I tried hard to fit in at Olivet, but it was really difficult since I was so different from everyone else. On the outside I looked like I was part of that community, but on the inside I was a very different person. Orval Baun saved me. Orval was the high school football coach and he asked if I would like to keep statistics for the football team. For the next two years, I went to every game and recorded tackles, passing yards, running yards, and the like. I tried out for school plays and got roles like Aunt Eller in Oklahoma. Evidently, I wasn't the type to get the guy, I guess. It got me through the smallness of the place. And, I don't mean in terms of actual size, I mean in mindedness, exposure to the world, interest in other ways of seeing things.

I struggled to stay in school and I spent a fair amount of time in the principal's office for insubordinate behavior. I almost didn't graduate because I had circulated a petition to allow girls to wear trousers to school. In 1969 we were only allowed to wear skirts or dresses—no more than four inches above the knee. And this was before the invention of pantyhose! I had a choice of either tearing up the petition (which all the girls had signed) or not graduate. I tore up the petition. The next year they changed the dress code.

- **Lesson Learned: Good ideas take time to germinate.**

In 1969 I went to Olivet College and really blossomed; it was a great place for me and it had a mission of social justice which appealed to me given that my life had been very globally oriented. I joined a sorority, was in drama productions, met great people, and continued taking stats for the men's sports teams—basketball, baseball, football, and wrestling. I was squarely in a man's world as the first female collegiate statistician in Michigan. I learned a lot about how to play that woman card! Just kidding! What card? We didn't even have ERA or Title IX. We were practically invisible.

- **Lesson Learned: Be smart and be visible.**

When I graduated from college, I went to work for a great man, Richard Letts, who was the Human Relations Director for the City of Lansing. I was assigned as the translator for community issues. But, I really wanted to be a teacher so I also looked for work in the Lansing School District. I thought my bilingualism might be a saleable skill. Mr. Letts remained my mentor for many years after.

- **Lesson Learned: Find good mentors.**

It was 1973 and Lansing had a fairly large migrant community and the school district needed teachers who spoke both English and Spanish. This is where I would meet people with whom I've remained friends for over four decades.

- **Lesson Learned: Lifelong friends are hard to find so hold them dear.**

While working at Grand River Elementary School, I met the person who would be my best friend, Betty Nichols, now Underwood. She drove a red Camaro, wore platform shoes and miniskirts, had a streak of peroxided blonde hair, and bright blue contact lenses. She was bright and cheery and she was a great teacher. I, on the other hand, drove a VW Van, wore sandals and bib overalls. My hair was in a long braid, eyes as brown as they are today. I was a revolutionary—it was the seventies after all and there was a lot of civil rights work to be done. And, I could speak Spanish with the kids and their families.

We ended up sitting at the same picnic table at the end-of-the-year party and she asked me, "So, what are you doing this summer?" To which I replied in my most "I'm so cool and you're not" voice, "I'm going to the Yucatan to see the Mayan ruins." "The Mayan ruins?!" she exclaimed excitedly. "Yeah," I said. "Wanna go?" "Yes, I'd love to!" Immediately I thought what on earth had I done? It was a challenge, not an invitation. Well that was in June of 1976 and ever since we've been best friends, each other's maids of honor, health advocate, travel partner when the husbands don't want to go, confidant, sister, and alter-ego. There's nothing greater than having a woman friend who stands with you through it all.

- **Lesson Learned: Sisterhood is a gift.**

And, by coincidence, that was the year I fell in love with Mr. Caamal Canul. Betty and I were visiting a small island off the coast of the Yucatan, Isla Mujeres. I saw this gorgeous man walking across the street and I asked the waiter who he was. He was the captain of one of the passenger ferries. So I followed him around for about three days—I think they call it stalking now. We became friends but after I returned home, I lost contact and for the next 12 years—and through a short but uncomfortable marriage—I never forgot him. I returned to the island in 1988 and found him again.

On May 24 of this year, we will celebrate our Silver Wedding Anniversary. He is the rudder, I am the sail. Our School Board refers to him as Saint Victor. The Caamal Canul is all his. As a Mayan, he is very proud of his ancestry and asked if I wouldn't mind taking his entire last name. When you're young and in love you agree to a lot of things that 25 years later you wonder what you were thinking! My husband once told me that my parents loved me too much. What did he mean by that? How could parents love their kids too much? He said that they gave me more confidence in myself than what the world is used to.

- **Lesson Learned: Believe in yourself. Set your sights on what you want and go for it–no matter how long it takes.**

Why I Wanted to Be an Educator

I suppose you can guess from the "who I am" section, why I would want to be a teacher. It just seemed as though there were so many kids who needed someone to listen to them, hear their hearts, find a place for them to be all they could be. I wanted to be that teacher that I wished I would have had. Someone who would have been cool with the apple tree or palm tree as an expression of self. I wanted to help create a safe place for kids to explore their talents, outside the roles that are sometimes ascribed to them by family or peers.

Having been raised in a very nontraditional way in a small family unit always wandering around the world, integrating into different cultures and languages, living between two worlds, I thought I could help those kids that were struggling to make sense of school and life. I wanted to make a difference and I wanted to be with kids in Lansing. For 27 years I was a teacher and principal in Lansing with great mentors like Eva Evans, Alda Henderson, Dick Halik, and Ben Perez. I retired in 2001 and went to other adventures but here I am 15 years later back on the path of my passion.

- **Lesson Learned: Do the work to where your heart leads you.**

I've had the good fortune of being involved in the enterprise of education my entire career. Either as a teacher, administrator, consultant, or in the corporate sector. I've been able to travel around the world—visiting and working in places like China, Japan, Bhutan, India, the Marshall Islands, Finland, Italy, Spain, México, Guatemala, Egypt, Kuwait, the United Arab Emirates. Through it all, what I have discovered is that kids are all the same. They have a dream of being someone special and to me, every one of them is.

- **Lesson Learned: It's a small world and we are much more alike than we are different.**

In order to make those dreams come true for kids, it's essential to have the best people working next to you. I am truly blessed to be among smart, capable, and caring women and men in the Lansing School District to help make our kids' dreams a reality.

- **Lesson Learned: Surround yourself with people who are smart, hard-working, and sane.**

Women in Leadership

Many years ago, women went to workshops that helped us enter into the professional ranks dominated by men. We were given tips on how to dress—blue suits. How to talk—be assertive, not passive. How to plan your career—10-year plans with benchmarks. How to maneuver the politics—go golfing. OK, so I didn't do any of those things. I never owned a blue suit, I did go to assertiveness training but it wasn't because of passivity. I didn't have a business plan that lasted more than "do I like what I'm doing? Or, am I ready to do something different?" I don't play golf, maybe I should take that up in retirement. My mom was a professional woman and I think I mostly learned from her, not a workshop.

- **Lesson Learned: Listen to the beat of your own drum.**

I began work at the age of 15 when my mom suggested I go clean tables at the local restaurant in Olivet to earn money to buy a blue shag coat I saw in the Penney's catalogue. At the time, I was pretty resentful that she wouldn't just buy it for me. But, it was probably the single best lesson I've learned—work and pay your way through life. She believed that relying on a husband for support was risky and beholding. She was right. Financial independence is foundational for women. It's what gives us the freedom to be all we can be. And, education is the key to opening the door to that freedom.

- **Lesson Learned: Never depend on someone else to support you.**

I've been a waitress, a cook's assistant—pastries and salads—and a bartender. At one point when I lived in Mexico for a year, I chauffeured fighting roosters from cockfight to cockfight. Now that was an interesting job! Little did I know then that it was a perfect training ground for my life as a superintendent. You meet all kinds of people in the cockfighting circuit and they all have a unique story.

- **Lesson Learned: No matter where you go, you'll find people greater and lesser than yourself–treat them as you would like to be treated.**

And, here I am today, with you. I'm just incredibly honored to have been asked to share pieces of my story. In the last 42 years as a professional woman, I continue to learn many lessons.

Leadership for All Seasons

- Be prepared to sacrifice yourself
- Be prepared to know yourself way better than you want to
- Know a lot about a lot
- Travel as much as you can
- Believe and act as if there are no enemies
- Dream, think, then do
- Take some risks, redesign the conventional
- Tell the people who work with you that they are the greatest
- Come to work earlier than anyone else, leave later than anyone else
- Set the expectation for excellence, then practice it
- Understand and believe that obstacles are sticky notes reminding you to go back, change direction, design
- Negotiate—find common ground whenever and wherever possible
- Practice PRAXIS
- Anticipate whenever possible, trust your intuition
- Gossip is a snake, be circumspect
- No one is "golden"—power shifts
- Your story is just that, your story, nothing more, nothing less
- Don't deprive anyone of their place, their time, their story
- Everything happens for a reason—*"cada perro tiene su día"*
- Be empathetic, especially when you don't feel like it
- Never apply for the same position in the same organization for which your supervisor is also applying. No matter the outcome, there will be a political price to pay.
- Don't "problem dump"
- Build professional equity and cash it in sparingly
- Build bridges, don't burn them—but make sure you cross them!

- Whenever you think you'll never do that, you will
- What goes around, comes around—so beware of what you send around
- Mentor people, work your way out of leadership
- Develop projects around people's strengths
- Organizational nihilism will disengage you slowly but surely
- Say "please" and "thank you" a lot, especially to wait staff
- Smile, enjoy life
- Watch the movies, *Babe*, *One Flew Over the Cuckoo's Nest*, *The Color Purple*, and *Meet John Doe* for a deeper understanding of leadership

References

- Blake, Robert and Jane Mouton. *Managerial Grid III: The Key to Leadership Excellence*. Gulf Publishing. 1964, 1978, 1985.

- Brenner, A. In an article in *Psychology Today*. Dr. Abigail Brenner, 2015.

- Castañeda, Carlos. *The Teachings of Don Juan: A Yaqui Way of Knowledge*. Balantine Books. 1968.

- Deal, Terrance and Alan Kennedy. *Corporate Cultures: The Rites and Rituals of Corporate Life*. Basic Books. 2000.

- Deal, Terrance and Kent Peterson. *Shaping School Culture*. Jossey-Bass. 2009.

- Derman-Sparks, Carol, Higa, Tanaka, and Sparks, Bill. "Children, Race and Racism: How Race Awareness Develops." 2014. www.teachingforchange.org

- DISC. accessed at: www.discprofile.com

- FIRO-B. accessed at: www.psychometrics.com

- Freire, Paulo. *Pedagogy of the Oppressed*. 1970.

- Gardner, Howard. *Five Minds for the Future*. Harvard Business Review Press. 2007.

- Gerzon, Mark. *Leading Through Conflict*. Harvard Business Review Press. 2006.

- Gino. F and M. Norton. Why Rituals Work. *Scientific American*. May 14, 2013.

- Goodlad, John. *A Place Called School*. McGraw-Hill. 1984.

- Hall, Edward. *The Silent Language*. Anchor Books. 1959.

- Hofstede, Geert and Hofstede, Gert. *Cultures and Organizations*. McGraw-Hill. 2005.

- Johari Window. accessed at: www.communicationtheory.org

- Justice, Tom and David Jamieson. *The Facilitator's Fieldbook*. Amacom. 1999.

- KAI. Kirton Adaption-Innovation Inventory. accessed at: www.kaicentre.com
- Keirsey, David and Marilyn Bates. *Please Understand Me*. Prometheus Nemesis. 1984.
- Knowles, M. S. (1973). *The adult learner: A neglected species*. Houston: Gulf Publishing Company. Revised Edition 1990.
- Kruse, Michael. Donald Trump Confronts a New Label: Loser. *Politico*. November 7, 2020.
- MBTI. Myers-Briggs Type Indicator. accessed at: www.myersbriggs.org
- O'Donnell, Wicklund, Pigozzi, and Peterson (OWP/P Architects) and Bruce Mau. *The Third Teacher*. 2010.
- Palmer, Parker. *Let Your Life Speak: Listening for the Voice of Vocation*. Jossey-Bass. 1999.
- Pearson, Carol. *The Hero Within*. HarperCollins. 1986.
- Phillips, Gary. Founder and President of National School Improvement Project, Inc.
- Thomas, David and Kerr Inkson. *Cultural Intelligence*. Berrett-Koehler Publishers. 2017.
- Tylor, E.B. *Primitive Culture: Researches Into the Development of Mythology, Philosophy, Religion, Art, and Custom*. John Murray. 1871.
- Rodgers, Richard. South Pacific. *You've Got to be Carefully Taught*. 1958
- Schein, Edgar. *Organizational Culture and Leadership*. John Wiley & Sons. 2017.
- Schein, Edgar. *Corporate Culture Survival Guide*. Jossey-Bass. 1999.
- Sinek, Simon. *Start with Why*. Portfolio. 2011.
- Useem, Ruth et al. (undated) "Third Culture Kids: Focus of Major Study". International Schools Services. Retrieved December 3, 2006.
- Wheatley, Margaret. *Leadership and the New Science: Discovering Order in a Chaotic World*. Berrett-Koehler. 2006.
- Wrzesniewski, A., N. LoBuglio, J. E. Dutton & J. M. Berg. Job Crafting and Cultivating Positive Meaning and Identity in Work. *Advances in Positive Organizational Psychology*. 2013, pp 281–302.

YVONNE CAAMAL CANUL (née Goudreault) has been an educator for over 45 years, serving in a wide variety of positions. Now retired from being an urban superintendent in Michigan, Yvonne is well known for spearheading numerous innovations, among them a classroom observation protocol named iCollaborate, a career and college pipeline known as the Pathway Promise, and the Flex Academy, a high school alternative learning schedule. Beyond her professional dedication, Yvonne has been recognized for her leadership. In 1982, Yvonne received the Irma Ramos Bilingual Educator of the Year awarded by the Michigan Education Association. In 1995, she was selected for the Milken National Educator Award. In 2006 the Michigan Education Association honored her with the David P. McMahon Civil Rights Award. In 2015, she was named Michigan's Superintendent of the Year, and in 2017 Yvonne was chosen to receive the National Women in School Leadership award from the American Association of School Administrators and the Bill and Melinda Gates Foundation. In 2019, the Lansing Regional Sister Cities Commission honored her with the Global Impact Award for her "Educational Leadership, Vision, and Pathways to Promise." Her degrees are from Michigan State University and Olivet College, which granted her an Honorary Doctorate in Humane Letters. Yvonne was raised in Brazil, México, and Chile, has traveled throughout the world, is fluent in Spanish, and is married to Victor Caamal Canul. Currently, Yvonne leads Caamal Canul Consulting, LLC and provides leadership and cultural competency training and coaching.

Made in the USA
Middletown, DE
07 January 2022

58021119R00124